I0759397

Bittersweet

The Five Tastes *of* Dessert *and* Beyond

HARVEST
An Imprint of WILLIAM MORROW

for beth / rest

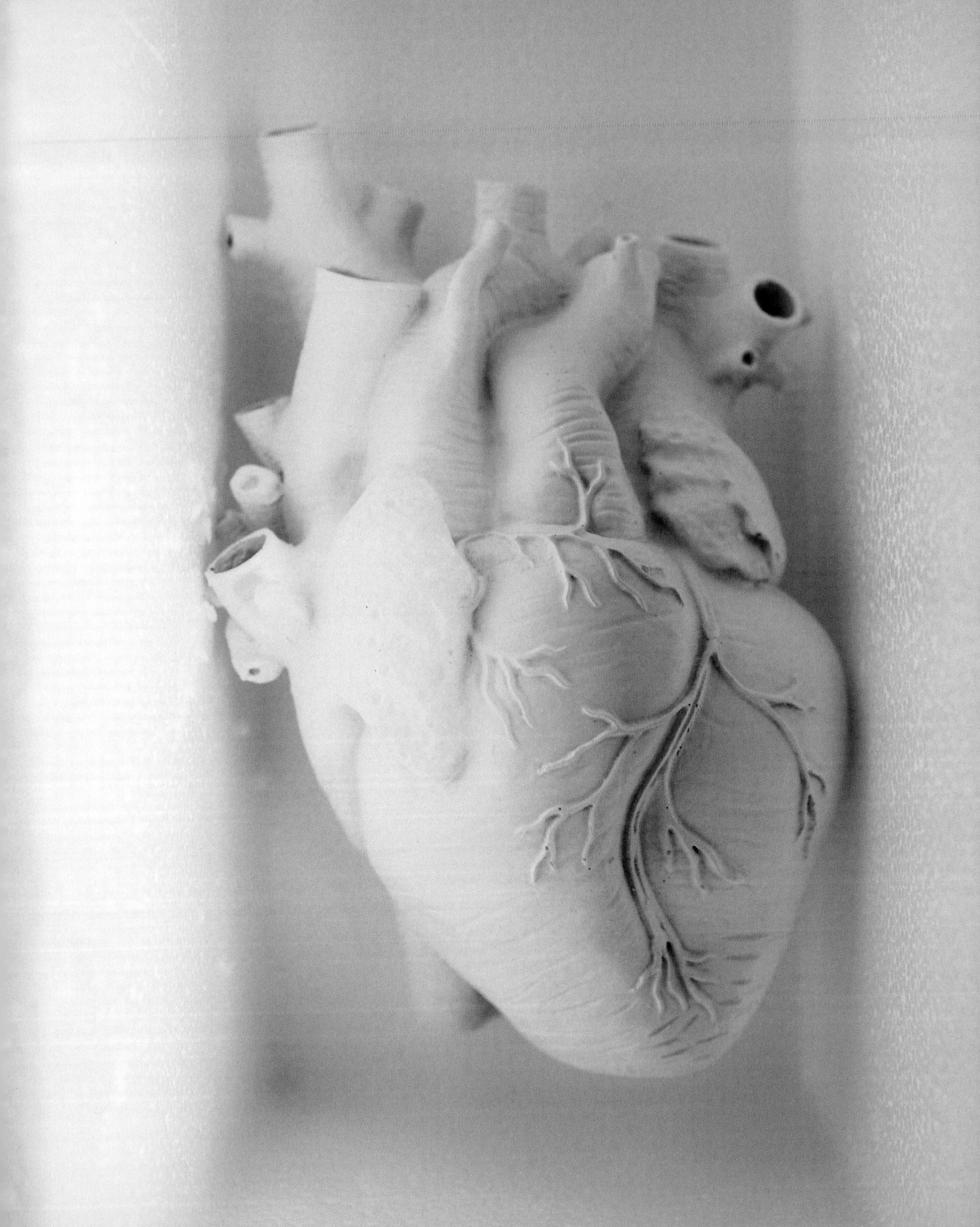

Should this be the end of the story?
A kind of sigh? A last ripple of the wave?
A trickle of water to some gutter
where, burbling, it dies away?
Let me touch the table—so—and thus
recover my sense of the moment.

—Virginia Woolf, *The Waves*

Recipes

Bitter

Sweet

Sour

Salt

Umami

WE HAVE FIVE TASTES, AND A SIXTH SENSE.

Bitter, Sweet, Sour, Salt, Umami—these universally agreed-upon words exist as transformational elements in dessert that, when harnessed, unite to form a more enticing experience of what we eat. But for all their weight, the exalted tastes transcend food—stirring both philosophical and physiological provocations. I will give you their classical definitions, and then I will give mine. Two meanings: one for your mouth, the other, your heart.

BITTER (*adj.*) *Having a sharp pungent taste or smell; not sweet.* Or a mouthful that's difficult to accept, receiving with distance whatever will come. Protective, reserved, and confronting, but not without hidden light.

SWEET (*adj.*) *Containing, or tasting as if it contains, a lot of sugar.* Pleasant, kind, and not considered harmful, mostly. A fine prospect of happiness.

SOUR (*adj.*) *Having a tart or acid taste, such as that which is characteristic of unripe fruits and vinegar.* At best, striking and defiant, filled with torrents of luminous clarity. At worst, to turn disagreeably. To avoid such taint by means of self-preservation; like a pucker that seeks consoling, or a shiver down the spine.

SALT (*noun*) *A white crystalline substance that gives seawater its characteristic taste and is used for seasoning or preserving food.* A familiar treatment that surpasses the shaker. To salt is to manufacture radiance or impart magnetism, drawing out moisture and forcing it in again, maintaining both separation and control. Wide, weathered, and geographical, this should be administered in considered doses.

UMAMI (*noun*) *The taste sensation that is produced by several amino acids and nucleotides (such as glutamate and aspartate) and has a rich or meaty flavor characteristic.* The satisfaction of our deepest cravings.

But the five tastes are far from linear or finished, for what we consider taste, really, is nothing more than a mixture of sensations. I can taste flavor, just as much as I can taste texture, sight, sound, or color—going deeper, emotion. I can taste my past, but easier my present when it's laid out on the table in front of me. I hope only to taste my future. That sixth sense of the beyond that transforms dessert exists inside us.

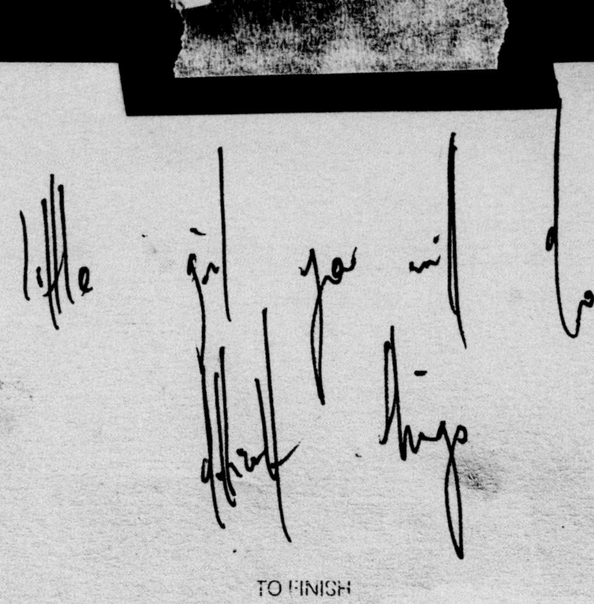

TO FINISH

section 28 monforte, riverine buffalo blue, pickled prune, oat crackers 24

mandarin sorbet, pepita caramel, coconut kefir 14

Jerusalem artichoke cream bun 12

please note a credit card surcharge may apply on your final bill

WHY DID YOU CHOOSE A MAN YOU

DID NOT TRUST?

An unapologetic sensualist at heart, the art of cooking is how I communicate and create, and my life experiences that extend past the palate, ultimately, end on the plate. Cooking is intuitive, as well as emotive, meditative, and healing. It's personal, a result of our cumulative essences, and the most beautiful part of it is creation. I often get carried away in this process and must call myself in. I look up to the five tastes to guide me, to bring to light the things I cannot yet see, but only feel, for that's the true role of the muse, or artist.

I believe that a memorable meal occurs at the intersection of taste and ourselves—my tastes are tinged with my sense, or vice versa, and these nuances are received on the tongue. Such connections play out on a deeper, subconscious level, which dessert can stimulate, altering both the mind and body. A mouthful can seem like a saving grace or enemy within, shifting from bitter to sweet and then back again, fast. Because dessert is transformational—not just constrained to a mouthful, but how during creation it can change.

Through side notes and reflections, these recipes speak of an intuitive instinct that can alter the last course—the sixth sense, if you will. And the five tastes constantly transform too. While sole and alone in themselves at the start, through sweetness, the tastes start to interact with each other, to commune, and take on new meaning. *Salt*, for example, never is just that. It can be marine, brackish, or sulfuric. In dessert, it offsets the sweet, strengthening but also inhibiting it, making the mouth salivate to want more. *Sour*, like a thorn in the thigh, has a harder time adjusting. It initially presents as citric, tangy, or tart, pure acid at the core, and can be used to stir things sickly-sweet to life. *Sugar* then is of importance, craved for comfort, connection, or calories, as much as it is critical to create. Similar can be said for *Umami*, which has a strong, life-affirming force that's meant to keep us at ease, and if the *Bitter* season of my life taught me anything—it's that one bite can prove fatal.

But I am not a scientist. I don't engage only in a practical world; forever one foot rooted in soil, the other stretching out to heaven. I don't have answers to chemicals, compounds, and structures, those clinical matters that seek to undress. What I am is a person, driven to the edge of understanding, so that ultimately we can eat better.

This book tells a tale of dessert through the spectrum of taste. And like all good fairy tales, it is light, it is dark, but it has a happy ending—those subconscious appetites that reside within you, and me, nourished. And there are tastes inside of us that we are yet to understand. Perhaps it is entirely conceivable that a slice of cake is best interpreted without words, or that a recipe can be constructed to call forth a reaction, to nurture a memory or even a wound, and then extend a healing hand. Because in the end, dessert is a sensual act, and I am in love with the mystery.

Bitter

i was warned about bitter—we all were. My grandmother, in all her loving glory, taught me not to seek out bitterness. I remember her seated across the table. Her hands, ink-blue veins, rippled and raised against her paper-thin skin. "Be sweet," she'd say. "Do as they tell you." ¶ But I have never done what I've been told. ¶ Like a moth to a flame, I am forever entranced with how we go hurling ourselves toward the thing that will hurt us. And what I discovered down that path is that sometimes a little unpleasantness is necessary. "A bitter pill to swallow," "to leave a bitter taste in the mouth," "a bittersweet end," all lessons learned in childhood. It took time for me to find the sweetness in those sentiments and accept that often the toxin and the cure are the same. ¶ For the word "bitter" belongs to more than taste. It's a sensation. A feeling, flavor, and circumstance. It has greater meaning to us than what can be experienced by the body alone. Bitter is a state of being. It can be strong, silent, even subservient, and it comes complete with its own moral code, refusing to obey any rule, law, or instruction, with a smirk. It doesn't seem kind at first, nor is it even meant to be eaten. To detect it is to detect a kind of poison—evolution tells us that. The throe of trepidation felt when we are confronted with bitterness is a warning—it's the intuitive senses screaming caution. The heart halts, then beats, faster. ¶ But a void exists that bitterness itself cannot fill. Bitter, sweet. Two halves that come together to form a whole, like soul mates. Divisive desires that serve one need in dessert, hunger. Each so alone in themselves but also so painfully connected, our lovers. Sometimes, this union can feel like a war, at others, harmony, for *amour* and *amer* don't just sound close together, they are. ¶ A lot of the time sugar can seem one dimensional; add bitterness, and it becomes complex. It brings clarity to cloy, it creates desire for more, and it's stimulating. I couldn't stomach a lot of bitterness before, but I came to understand, however unwilling. I'd like to thank age and time for that, but I think it's more innate. Put simply, bitter is not a taste we naturally take to, though it is enticing. At first, the dark taunt seems unpleasant, but with some treatment and consoling, easily, it becomes lovable. It shows us that something long thought of as harsh can, too, be beautiful. It's the most wonderful sense I know; delicate and fragile yet biting. ¶ This chapter is dedicated to that bite. Revealing, releasing, and reclaiming the volatile thing the protective part of our bodies tells us we shouldn't. ¶ Like a wound, bitter leaves its mark.

The Dark Side Roulade

FOR THE SPONGE

⅔ cup + 2 tablespoons (60 g) Dutch processed cocoa powder, sifted, plus more for dusting

2 tablespoons unsalted butter, melted

6 large eggs, separated

¾ cup (150 g) granulated sugar

A pinch of salt

FOR THE CREAM FILLING

⅔ cup (80 g) confectioners' sugar

⅓ cup + 1 tablespoon (30 g) Dutch processed cocoa powder

1 cup (240 g) mascarpone

¾ cup (180 ml) heavy cream

A shot of espresso

1 teaspoon vanilla extract

⅔ cup (115 g) melted dark chocolate

Dutch processed cocoa powder, for dusting

From the outside, a roulade seems fragile—this one has bite. Fragments of dark chocolate sheath the inside, which are revealed only upon slicing, and take the mouth by surprise. It gives this classically austere sponge and cream roll structure, rigor, and restraint, but, most importantly, something to sink your teeth in.

/ *Serves 6 to 8* /

Preheat the oven with the rack in the middle to 350°F (180°C). Grease and line a 13 x 9 x 1-inch (32 x 23 x 2.5-cm) rimmed quarter sheet pan. Lightly grease the paper too.

To make the sponge, stir together the cocoa powder, butter, and ⅓ cup (80 ml) hot water in a small bowl until a smooth paste has formed.

In the bowl of a stand mixer that's fitted with the whisk attachment, whisk the egg yolks with ½ cup (100 g) of the sugar on medium-high speed until pale, thick, and voluminous, about 5 minutes. Scrape in the cocoa paste and whisk until well combined.

In a separate bowl, whisk the egg whites and salt on medium speed to soft and foamy peaks. Scatter in the remaining ¼ cup (50 g) sugar, a little at a time, until it's all used up. Continue to whisk until the meringue is thick and glossy, being careful not to overwork it to stiff clumps. With a large rubber spatula, fold a third into the bowl with the chocolate mixture to loosen, followed by another third until just combined, and then the last. Scrape into the prepared pan, tenderly smoothing it out to the edges with an offset palette knife.

Bake for 18 to 22 minutes, until the sponge springs back when lightly pressed and has just started to shrink away from the sides of the pan. Set onto a wire cooling rack, then dust the surface with enough cocoa to lightly coat. Cover with a clean kitchen towel. Flip to invert, then peel off the paper. With the help of the towel, roll the sponge up from the shortest side. Leave to cool completely in the sling, seam facing down.

To make the cream filling, sift the confectioners' sugar and cocoa powder into the bowl of a stand mixer. Add the mascarpone, cream, espresso, and vanilla. Whisk on medium speed until smooth, thick, and spreadable.

Unroll the sponge onto a cutting board. Slick the surface thinly with melted chocolate. Spread over the cream (you may not wish to use all of it), then reroll. It's fine, if not ideal, if it splits. Neaten off the edges with a sharp serrated knife, then transfer the roulade to a plate. Chill for an hour or so, until the middle has firmed, before serving.

This is best eaten on the day of making.

Fernet Ice Cream and Feuilletine

FOR THE ICE CREAM

2 cups (480 ml) heavy cream

1½ cups (360 ml) whole milk

A thick strip of orange peel

5 large egg yolks

⅔ cup (135 g) granulated sugar

¼ cup (30 g) skim milk powder

1 teaspoon vanilla extract

3 tablespoons fernet

FOR THE FEUILLETINE

½ cup + 1 tablespoon (70 g) all-purpose flour

3 tablespoons Dutch processed cocoa powder

A pinch of salt

⅓ cup + 1 tablespoon (90 g) unsalted butter, softened at room temperature

½ cup + 1 tablespoon (115 g) granulated sugar

1 large egg white

3 tablespoons brewed coffee, cooled

It was once posed to me that the fact that alcohol won't freeze is as much a philosophical question as a scientific one. It is true that the ethanol in this recipe interferes with the firming process, creating a mouthfeel that's more willing and pliant, but not without sting.

Fernet, falling under the classification of amaro, is a substance of style. The kind used will affect the finish of this ice cream. My favorite, from Austria, is on the lighter side, and made with roots, herbs, and spices found in the forest during hunting season. I think it lends a tale of primality to this dessert; the deer in the headlights unfreezes and gets away.

/ *Serves 4* /

To make the ice cream base, put the cream, milk, and peel in a large and heavy-bottomed saucepan. Bring to a simmer over medium heat. Meanwhile, in a medium heatproof bowl, whisk together the egg yolks, sugar, skim milk powder, and vanilla until thick and pale. Slip a ladle of the hot liquid into the bowl with the yolks, whisking continuously as it's added, then whisk in another until combined. Pour back into the pan that's set on the stove. Continue to heat, stirring slowly, until the mixture is thick enough to coat the back of a spoon, 5 to 6 minutes. If you have a thermometer, it should fall within an optimal range of 170°F to 180°F (77°C to 82°C). Remove from the heat and stir in the fernet. Strain through a fine-mesh sieve into a large heatproof bowl, then cover with plastic wrap. Chill for at least 8 hours, but preferably overnight.

When you're ready to churn, place a container or aluminum loaf pan in the freezer to keep cold. Pour the chilled ice cream base into an ice cream machine. Churn according to the manufacturer's instructions. It'll be thick, aerated, and doubled in volume when it's done. Extract into the par-frozen container, then cover with aluminum foil and freeze for a few hours, until just firm.

To make the feuilletine, adjust racks to the top and bottom thirds of the oven and preheat it to 350°F (180°C). Line two large baking sheets with parchment paper.

Sift the flour, cocoa powder, and salt into a medium bowl.

In the bowl of a stand mixer that's fitted with the paddle attachment, or using handheld electric beaters, beat the butter and sugar together on medium speed until creamy but not aerated. Pause to scrape down the bowl, then beat in the egg white to emulsify. Lower the speed and beat in the dry ingredients, followed by the coffee. Raise the speed slightly. Continue to beat for a minute or so, until well combined, almost like frosting. Divide between the prepared sheets, smoothing out the sticky mass with an offset palette knife into an ultra-thin layer.

Bake for 7 to 9 minutes, rotating halfway through, until dry. Leave to cool and crisp on the sheets before roughly breaking apart.

Serve the shards piercing the ice cream. This will keep, covered, in the coldest part of the freezer for about a week, but the feuilletine should be sealed in an airtight container and stored in a cool, dark place.

Burnt Sage Streusel Cake

Though most often used for savory, sage adores sweetness. The nuances vary from leaf to leaf, presenting as woodsy, musky, peppery, or astringent, but what doesn't change is sage's unmistakable strength. As such, it should be worked with sparingly, and in desserts that can handle it. A streusel cake is known to withstand treatment, and a great one has a harsh crust to protect the tender interior. I like to glaze it with something bitter and burnt to complete the contrast.

/ *Serves 9* /

FOR THE STREUSEL

1 cup (125 g) all-purpose flour

⅓ cup (75 g) light brown sugar

3 tablespoons granulated sugar

2 teaspoons ground cinnamon

1 teaspoon Dutch processed cocoa powder

¼ teaspoon ground cloves

A pinch of salt

⅓ cup + 1 tablespoon (90 g) unsalted butter, melted

⅓ cup (45 g) walnuts, chopped

FOR THE CAKE

⅓ cup (45 g) walnuts

1½ cups + 1 teaspoon (190 g) all-purpose flour

1¼ teaspoons baking powder

¼ teaspoon salt

½ cup + 1 tablespoon (130 g) unsalted butter, softened at room temperature

¾ cup (150 g) granulated sugar

2 large eggs

2 teaspoons vanilla extract

1 cup (240 g) sour cream

FOR THE GLAZE

1½ cups (180 g) confectioners' sugar

¼ cup (60 g) unsalted butter, cubed

3 sage leaves

Whole milk, to thin

ADJUST a rack to the middle of the oven, then preheat it to 350°F (180°C). Grease and line an 8-inch (20-cm) square baking pan with parchment paper, leaving a slight sling over the sides.

To make the streusel, in a large mixing bowl, whisk together the flour, sugars, cinnamon, cocoa powder, cloves, and salt. Pour in the butter, then stir to form evenly moistened crumbles. Stir in the walnuts. Set aside while you prepare the cake batter.

Scatter the walnuts into an even layer on a lined baking sheet. Roast for 8 to 10 minutes, until golden brown and fragrant. Cool, then transfer to a food processor or grinder and blitz to a meal, stopping short of damp clumps. Tip into a large mixing bowl, then sift over the flour, baking powder, and salt. Whisk to combine.

In the bowl of a stand mixer that's fitted with the paddle attachment, or using handheld electric beaters, beat the butter and sugar on medium speed until light and fluffy, 3 to 5 minutes. Pause to scrape down the bowl, then beat in the eggs, one at a time, incorporating well after each addition. Beat in the vanilla, then lower the speed. Beat in half of the dry ingredients, followed by all of the sour cream, and then the last of the dry ingredients, until well combined. Scrape the batter into the prepared pan, smoothing it out to the edges with an offset palette knife. Pile on the streusel.

Bake for just over an hour, until golden brown and a skewer inserted into the middle comes out clean. Let the cake cool in the pan for 15 minutes, then lift it out and onto a wire rack to cool completely.

To glaze, sift the confectioners' sugar into a medium bowl. Put the butter and sage into a small saucepan, then set it over medium-high heat. Stir until melted. Raise the heat and continue to cook, swirling the pan often but without stirring, until a nutty brown liquid has formed. It will foam, hiss, and crackle, but subside as it nears done. Fish out the leaves,

the sixth sense

You can alter the potency of this cake further with herbs, including additional sage, into the batter. Sometimes I'll rub the leaves into the sugar to free their rich fumes and wreck the downy structure. It adds a fattening to the crumb too, or so it seems.

setting them aside to cool and crisp on a paper towel, then pour the burnt butter into the sugar, whisking to combine. Whisk in a spoonful of milk at a time until the glaze is smooth, thick, and glossy—it shouldn't need more than 2 tablespoons. Glaze the cake and adorn with the reserved leaves. Leave to set, then slice and serve.

This is best eaten on the day of making, but will keep, stored in an airtight container, at room temperature for 3 days.

Cracked Chocolate Cookies

- 1½ cups (255 g) chopped dark chocolate
- ⅓ cup + 1 teaspoon (80 g) unsalted butter, cubed
- ⅓ cup + 1 teaspoon (45 g) all-purpose flour
- ⅓ cup (25 g) Dutch processed cocoa powder
- 1 teaspoon coffee powder
- ½ teaspoon baking powder
- ¼ teaspoon salt
- 1¼ cups (250 g) granulated sugar
- 2 large eggs

I can't stress enough the importance of letting these crack. The dough is delicate to handle at first; sticky, soft, and supple, almost formless, but the structure pulls together seamlessly at the end. It's all part of the process, and the result is the most beautiful and brooding ganache-like cookie that's not for the faint of heart.

/ ***Makes 16 cookies*** /

Put the chocolate and butter into a medium heatproof bowl, then set it over a saucepan that's filled with a few inches of barely simmering water. Do not let the base of the bowl touch the water below. Heat, stirring slowly, until melted. Remove and set aside until needed.

Sift together the flour, cocoa powder, coffee, baking powder, and salt into a medium mixing bowl.

In the bowl of a stand mixer that's fitted with the whisk attachment, whisk the sugar and eggs on medium-high speed until pale, thick, and almost doubled in volume, about 3 minutes. Lower the speed, then stream in the chocolate mixture, whisking until no dark streaks remain. Tip in the dry ingredients and whisk until almost combined, then finish mixing with a large spatula and a few turns of the hand to ensure that it's even. The dough should be soft and thick, leaving a flowing trail. Cover and chill in the refrigerator for about half an hour, to slightly firm.

Meanwhile, adjust racks to the top and bottom thirds of the oven, then preheat it to 350°F (180°C). Line two baking sheets with parchment paper.

Using a medium 2¾-inch (7-cm) scoop, portion the dough into even-sized mounds onto the sheets, leaving a few inches of space apart for spreading. It will be sticky and hard to handle but hold its shape. I find that dipping the scoop into a glass of warm water, and cleaning it off often, is helpful for neater portioning.

Bake for 12 to 14 minutes, rotating halfway through, until puffed, cracked, and the edges are set. The middle should retain a hefty squidge. Leave to cool on the sheets for a few minutes, then lift off and onto a wire rack to cool further before serving. The cookies will soften slightly with time but become more intense—an oxymoron. They'll keep well, stored in an airtight container at room temperature, for about 3 days.

the sixth sense

My instinct here is not taste led, but visual. Kintsugi, the art of making broken fractures whole, can transform these cookies—as in edible gold applied into the cracks.

Oil, Chocolate, and Bread

4 thick slices of bread

½ cup (85 g) finely chopped dark chocolate

Extra-virgin olive oil

Coarse sea salt

I can't claim my darkest desires. This belongs to Chef Ferran Adrià, of El Bulli fame, though the methodology has changed. It's the spark of genius, a bare-bones recipe, and one that I've returned to often. Under intense heat, the chocolate should battle itself in the oven. It's tempting to reach for it, to soothe it, and let it slick your tongue, your fingers. But resist—the scorch is the point.

/ *Serves 4* /

Preheat the oven to 400°F (200°C). Line a baking sheet with parchment paper and place the bread on the parchment, spacing each piece apart. Divide the chocolate, scattering it evenly over the slices.

Roast for 10 to 12 minutes, until the heart of the chocolate has disintegrated and the edges have darkened. You'll smell a scorch. Remove from the oven and smear it out with a knife. Drizzle with enough oil and flourish with salt. Eat before it has a chance to harden.

the sixth sense

Dark bread, like rye, will give this a greater pronounced bitterness.

Buckwheat Mousse

FOR THE MOUSSE

1½ cups (255 g) chopped dark chocolate

½ cup + 2 tablespoons (150 ml) heavy cream

2 large egg yolks

4 large egg whites

A pinch of salt

⅓ cup (70 g) granulated sugar

FOR THE CRACK TOP

2 tablespoons raw buckwheat groats

½ cup (85 g) chopped dark chocolate

the sixth sense

Though texturally light, there's little reprieve from bitterness in this mousse. I place a bowl of crème fraîche on the table when serving it to adjust the intensity as necessary.

This is a mousse that seems simple on the surface, but what lies beneath is complex. The process is a little different from other recipes, but it's one that I prefer. There are some things to flag. The first is in the heating of the chocolate and cream. Leave it alone, mostly, then stir until just melted, or risk splitting. If it does, that's fine—it can be rectified and continued on with. But time, through exposure to heat, is of the essence. The second is in your folding. Mousse is all about that lovely aeration, and we want to retain as much of it as possible. Try to fold with as few turns of the hand as possible. I follow the arch of the bowl and work inward, softening with each stroke. And, finally, the chocolate. I use a couverture with a cocoa solid of no more than 70%, which is intense but without the overwhelm.

/ *Serves 6 to 8* /

To make the mousse, put the chocolate and cream into a medium heatproof bowl, then set it over a saucepan that's filled with a few inches of barely simmering water. Do not let the base of the bowl touch the water below. Stir over medium-low heat until melted. Remove and whisk in the yolks, doing no more than necessary to get the mixture thick, glossy, and homogenous.

In the bowl of a stand mixer that's fitted with the whisk attachment, whisk the egg whites and salt on medium speed to foamy peaks. Scatter in the sugar, a little at a time, until it's all used up. Continue to whisk until the meringue stands in glossy-thick peaks. With a rubber spatula, fold a third into the chocolate mixture to loosen it, followed by another third until just incorporated, then the last. Transfer into your desired vessel, gently smoothing it out and being cautious of deflation. Chill for at least 4 hours.

Once the mousse has developed a backbone to support weight, make the crack top. Toast the buckwheat groats in a dry skillet over medium heat, shaking often, until deeply fragrant. Set aside to cool. Next, melt down the chocolate in a double boiler. Remove and stir in the groats. Spread the mixture all over the chilled mousse. It'll start to set as soon as it hits the surface, so be fast and precise with your dispersion. Chill for a few more hours, until hard.

Fracture the mousse at the table, then serve. It will keep, covered, in the refrigerator for 2 to 3 days.

Glazed Grapefruit Suzette

FOR THE CRÊPES

3 tablespoons unsalted butter, plus more for cooking the crêpes

1¼ cups (155 g) all-purpose flour

2 tablespoons granulated sugar

¼ teaspoon salt

3 large eggs

Seeds scraped from 1 vanilla bean

1½ cups (360 ml) whole milk

FOR THE GLAZED GRAPEFRUIT

1 grapefruit

¼ cup (50 g) granulated sugar

1 teaspoon salt

FOR THE SAUCE

⅔ cup (135 g) granulated sugar

¾ cup (170 g) unsalted butter, cubed

¾ cup (180 ml) freshly squeezed grapefruit juice

Juice from ½ a lemon

¼ cup (60 ml) amaro

2 tablespoons brandy, like Cognac

Crêpes Suzette is known for self-extinguishment, or so the story goes. Fire refines the flavor, turning it intense and layered, but most importantly to this version, de-bittered.

The amaro that forms part of the ignition isn't traditional but chosen to evoke a sense of place. The kind I use is balanced with a unique blend of Australian citrus, herbs, and florals, and is ruby-jewel-toned, like ochre. Grand Marnier is considered the classic choice, and it will take you far as it once did for me, but also someplace else.

Let the flames reflect your spirit.

/ *Serves 4* /

First, burn the butter for the crêpes. Place it into a medium saucepan. Set it over medium-high heat and stir until melted. Raise the heat and continue to cook, swirling the pan often but without stirring, until a nutty brown liquid has formed. It will foam, hiss, and crackle, but subside as it nears done. Pour into a large heatproof bowl, scraping in any burnt bits. Sift in the flour, then add the sugar, salt, eggs, and vanilla. Whisk to incorporate, then stream in the milk, whisking slowly, until combined. It should be similar to the consistency of pouring cream. Pass the batter through a fine-mesh sieve into a separate bowl, then cover and leave to rest on the kitchen counter for an hour.

Next, make the glazed grapefruit. Use a peeler to remove the rind, avoiding the pith. Slice ultra-thin, then segment the rest of the fruit, leaving it aside. Put the rind into a medium saucepan and cover with cold water. Bring to a boil, then strain. Repeat this process twice more. Add the sugar and salt to the pan, along with ⅓ cup (80 ml) water. Cook over medium heat, swirling the pan occasionally, until translucent. Fish out the strands, separating them onto a lined baking sheet. Set aside.

When you're ready to cook, give the rested batter a gentle stir to awaken it. Set a 10-inch (25-cm) crêpe pan over medium heat and slick it with butter. Stream in a scant ⅓ cup of batter, raising and swirling the pan as you pour, so that a thin film lines the base. Cook for 1 to 2 minutes, until light golden. It'll tell you when it's time to flip, with some phantom movements that disrupt the surface. Flip, and cook the other side for about a minute more. Fold the crêpe into quarters. Transfer it to a plate, wipe the pan, re-butter, and repeat with the remaining batter. Tent the crêpes with aluminum foil and keep warm.

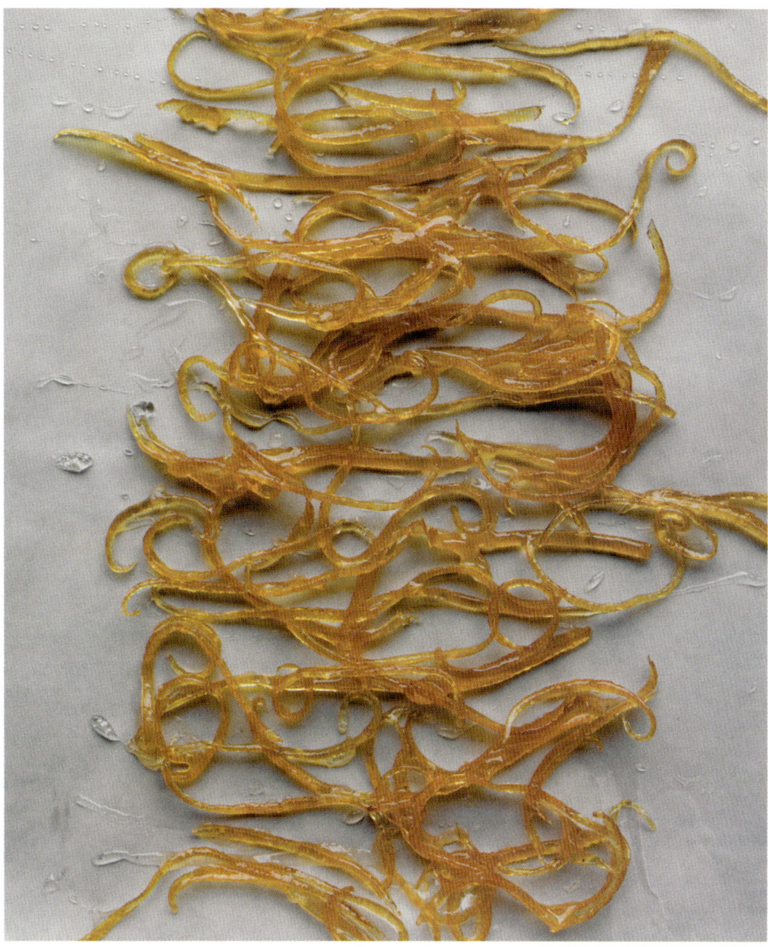

To make the sauce, set a large cast-iron skillet over medium-high heat and scatter over the sugar. Cook, disturbing often, until caramelized. Add the butter, shaking, swirling, and spinning it around to combine. Let it bubble and turn amber, a few minutes. Add the citrus juices and a handful of the glazed grapefruit. Continue to cook until the bubbling sauce has reduced and thickened slightly.

Lay the crêpes into the pan, overlapping them to fit. Wiggle in the sauce. Carefully pour in the amaro and brandy. Take a tentative step back from the pan and ignite the fumes with a long match or lighter. Lower the heat. The flames will self-extinguish as the alcohol cooks out. Turn off the heat and settle for a moment.

Serve warm, soon after, lashed with sauce. Top with more glazed grapefruit and the reserved segments, if desired—vanilla ice cream on the side never goes astray either.

Brittle Truffles

FOR THE BRITTLE

½ cup (70 g) roasted almonds

½ cup (100 g) granulated sugar

FOR THE GANACHE

1 cup + 2 tablespoons (190 g) finely chopped dark chocolate

¾ cup (180 ml) heavy cream

2 tablespoons unsalted butter

FOR COATING

⅔ cup (50 g) Dutch processed cocoa powder

1⅓ cups (230 g) finely chopped dark chocolate

This brittle is wet. It'll cook out slow until most of the liquid has left and all that remains is a sticky sap that knows little kindness. And then in go the almonds, an attempt at relief. Yield to the temptation to let it be too light. We're taught to be cautious of dark things, but these truffles will have you questioning that.

/ *Makes 32 to 36 truffles* /

Line a baking sheet with parchment paper, then set it near the space where you'll be working.

To make the brittle, scatter the almonds over the prepared baking sheet into an even layer. Put the sugar and ¼ cup (60 ml) water into a medium saucepan. Cook over medium-high heat, swirling occasionally but not stirring, until dark amber in hue. It will take some time to turn, but don't abandon it, as things change fast. Pour over the almonds and leave to harden.

Break the brittle into shards, then measure or weigh it—you'll need about ⅓ cup (50 g) for this recipe. Transfer to a food processor and blitz to a fine dust.

Next, for the ganache, place the chocolate into a medium heatproof bowl. In a small saucepan, bring the cream and butter to a simmer over gentle heat, then stream it all over the chocolate. Stand for a minute, then stir until smooth. Fold in the brittle. Leave on the kitchen counter until the ganache is thick enough to pipe, stirring it occasionally. It should take less than an hour in a cool climate, a little longer if not. If it's humid, I'll put the bowl in the refrigerator and stir every 5 minutes or so until done—but opt for the slow and controlled method if you can.

Transfer the ganache to a plastic piping bag and snip an inch off the tip. Twist tight, and, with some pressure, pipe it out and into long lines down a lined baking sheet. Refrigerate until firm enough to handle, about an hour.

With a sharp knife, slice the lines into truffles that are 2 inches (5 cm) in length, cleaning the knife each time you cut. Set aside while you sift the cocoa powder into a small bowl. Melt the chocolate down over a double boiler.

Dip the truffles into the chocolate, shake off the excess, then return them to the sheet. The residual coldness will set the coating. Rattle each liberally in cocoa. I use my hands for this part—it'll be messy but efficient, and you'll develop a systematic flair as you go.

Serve the truffles at room temperature. They can be sealed in an airtight container and stored in the refrigerator, to be eaten within a week.

Croissant French Toast

4 very good croissants

4 large eggs

½ cup (100 g) granulated sugar, plus more for sprinkling

Seeds scraped from 1 vanilla bean

1¼ cups (300 ml) whole milk

⅓ cup (80 ml) heavy cream

Two shots of espresso, cooled

Salted butter, for cooking the croissants

It's a lover's thing to start the morning with coffee and croissants, and though I am nothing if not willing, I'm not the best at making either from scratch. French toast is the way I oblige. The sugar at the end is the best part. It caramelizes over heat, and as it cools, sets to a crisp. I still relinquish the role of coffee maker but sometimes steal the grinds to add into the custard for a more toothed grit.

/ ***Serves 2 to 4*** /

HALVE the croissants with a sharp serrated knife, handling them with care to avoid tearing their delicate webbing.

In a large mixing bowl, whisk together the eggs, sugar, and vanilla seeds. Pour in the milk, cream, and espresso. Whisk slowly until combined. Pour the custard into a rimmed dish. Soak the croissant halves, turning them over a few times, until absorbed. Set aside onto a double-lined baking sheet.

Position a large frying pan over medium-high heat. Add a pat of butter and swirl it around until melted. Fit in as many croissants as feel comfortable. They will be tender by this point, so be gentle. Cook for about 3 minutes, until the bases are golden brown, adjusting the heat as necessary. Sprinkle with a pinch of sugar, then flip. Cook until caramelized all over, about 2 more minutes. Eat soon after, hot.

Pecan Financiers

¾ cup (105 g) pecans

½ cup + 1 teaspoon (65 g) all-purpose flour

⅓ cup + 1 teaspoon (35 g) almond meal

1 teaspoon coffee powder

¼ teaspoon salt

1 cup (200 g) granulated sugar

4 large egg whites

⅓ cup + 1 tablespoon (90 g) unsalted butter, melted and cooled

the sixth sense

Brown off ¼ cup (60 g) butter in a small saucepan over the stove, swirling it around until tinged. Pour it into a medium heatproof bowl, scraping in any residual burnt bits. Add 1 cup (120 g) sifted confectioners' sugar, as well as a slip of vanilla extract. Whisk to incorporate. The glaze will be stiff, then add enough milk until it reaches your desired consistency. Mine is thick but pourable. Dip in the financiers, adorning the tops with a roasted pecan.

The bitter phenolics of a pecan are the perfect foil for a cake that's built on sugar. Roasting brings out the pecan's bite, creating a sultry smoke show that ignites all the senses. Opinions differ on how a financier should be finished—glazed or not. I've listed a burnt coating at the end of this. It's a gild, but a great one.

/ ***Makes 12 financiers*** /

Adjust a rack to the middle of the oven, then preheat it to 350°F (180°C). Grease a twelve-hole bar mold for financiers. Line a baking sheet with parchment paper, then scatter the pecans over it. Roast for 10 to 12 minutes, until browned and fragrant. Cool, then blitz to a meal in a food processor, stopping short of damp clumps.

In a large mixing bowl, whisk together the ground pecans, flour, almond meal, coffee powder, and salt. Stir in the sugar. Give the egg whites a good stir to loosen, then whisk them into the dry ingredients. The mixture will be very thick. Whisk in the butter until uniform. Spoon into the molds, filling almost to the top.

Bake for about 25 minutes, rotating halfway through, until golden, bumped, and split. Remove and cool for a few minutes, then release the financiers from the molds onto a wire rack. They can be served warm but are best near or at room temperature. These will keep, stored in an airtight container, at room temperature for 3 to 5 days.

Oatmeal and Peel Cookies

1¾ cups + 1½ tablespoons (230 g) all-purpose flour

1 teaspoon ground cardamom

½ teaspoon baking powder

¼ teaspoon baking soda

½ teaspoon salt

3⅓ cups + 1 teaspoon (270 g) rolled oats

¾ cup + 2 tablespoons (200 g) unsalted butter, softened at room temperature

1 cup + 2 tablespoons (250 g) light brown sugar

1 cup (200 g) granulated sugar

2 large eggs

1 tablespoon vanilla extract

Zest from ½ an orange

⅔ cup (115 g) chopped dark chocolate

½ cup (80 g) diced candied citrus peel

Flaky sea salt, for finishing

Confectioners' sugar, for dusting

the sixth sense

Most people have thoughts on the ideal oatmeal cookie. I'm no purist, and sometimes swap the candied citrus peel for cherries, which take these from bitter to sour, fast. If you want to alter them too, use no more than ⅓ cup of anything.

The bitter in citrus is contained within the peel, pith, and pips—all the typically discarded parts, like the membrane that holds the fruit together and keeps it from coming apart, undone. I often rely on the skin for flavor, finding it luminous and striking, ideal to clarify anything sweet. The peel used in these textural cookies isn't lost, and travels far.

/ *Makes 28 cookies* /

In a large mixing bowl, whisk together the flour, cardamom, baking powder, baking soda, and salt. Stir in the oats.

In the bowl of a stand mixer that's fitted with the paddle attachment, or using handheld electric beaters, beat the butter and sugars on medium speed until creamy and light caramel in color, 3 to 5 minutes. Pause to scrape down the bowl, then beat in the eggs, followed by the vanilla and zest. Set the speed to low, then tip in the dry ingredients. Beat until incorporated, then beat in the chocolate and candied citrus peel until evenly distributed. Cover and chill until the dough is firm enough to handle, about 30 minutes.

Adjust racks to the top, middle, and bottom thirds of the oven, then preheat it to 350°F (180°C). Line three baking sheets with parchment paper.

Using a medium 2¾-inch (7-cm) scoop or heaping tablespoon as a measure, portion out even-sized amounts from the dough, rolling into balls with the palms of your hands. Divide among the prepared sheets, fitting on as many as possible, and making sure to leave a few inches of space apart for spreading. Set any leftovers aside to be baked off later, or store in an airtight container and freeze for up to 3 months. Sprinkle the tops with salt.

Bake for 13 to 15 minutes, rotating halfway through, until golden brown. Leave on the sheets for a few minutes, before lifting off and onto a wire rack to cool completely. Once cool, dust lightly with confectioners' sugar—I like to keep part of the cookies stark, for one sweet side and the other more bitter. Serve, soon after. These will keep, stored in an airtight container at room temperature, for about 3 days.

Grand Marnier Soufflés

FOR THE BASE

1 cup (240 ml) whole milk

1 teaspoon vanilla extract

A pinch of freshly grated nutmeg and orange zest

3 large egg yolks

¼ cup (50 g) granulated sugar

¼ cup + 2 teaspoons (37 g) all-purpose flour

2 tablespoons Grand Marnier

FOR THE CREAM

⅔ cup (160 ml) heavy cream

1 tablespoon Grand Marnier

2 teaspoons confectioners' sugar

FOR THE SOUFFLÉS

Unsalted butter, melted, for greasing

2 tablespoons granulated sugar, plus more for coating

4 large egg whites, at room temperature

Confectioners' sugar, to finish

the sixth sense

The distilled taste of Grand Marnier pairs well with marmalade, as they share a similar bitter, sweet, and old-world profile. I like to sink spoonfuls of the sticky substance into the cavities of each soufflé for an astringent edge.

Despite their ethereal nature, soufflés can withstand bold treatment. The linear bitterness of Grand Marnier is the greatest liqueur to bolster both flavor and nostalgia, and I remember it well, spoonfuls deep at Bistro Paul Bert in Paris.

Here, timing is key. Breath is the start and end of all soufflés—eat as soon as they exit.

/ *Serves 4* /

For the base, put the milk, vanilla, nutmeg, and zest into a medium saucepan and bring to a simmer over gentle heat. Meanwhile, whisk together the yolks, sugar, and flour until pale in a heatproof bowl. Stream a little of the hot milk into the yolks, whisking to incorporate, then transfer it all back into the pan that's set on the stove. Continue to heat, whisking continuously, until the custard is smooth and thick. Remove and whisk in the Grand Marnier. Pass through a fine-mesh sieve into a medium heatproof bowl, then cover the surface with with plastic wrap. Chill completely.

Before you plan to bake, in the bowl of a stand mixer that's fitted with the whisk attachment, whip the cream, Grand Marnier, and confectioners' sugar on medium speed to soft peaks. Keep cold until needed.

Adjust a rack to the middle of the oven, then preheat it to 375°F (190°C). Grease four 6¾-ounce (200-ml) capacity ramekins with butter, brushing it on in upward strokes. Scatter in sugar to coat, then tap out the excess. Set the ramekins onto a baking sheet.

In the bowl of a stand mixer that's fitted with the whisk attachment, whisk the egg whites on medium speed until foamy. Sprinkle in the sugar, without flooding it. Continue to whisk until thick and glossy peaks have formed. Remove the custard base from the refrigerator and give it a stir to loosen. Fold in a third of the meringue until almost combined, followed by another third, and then the last, becoming gentler with each stroke. Divide among the ramekins and level out the tops with an offset palette knife. Run your finger around the edges to make a lip so the soufflés aren't hindered from rising up.

Bake for 13 to 14 minutes, until risen and browned, resisting the temptation to open the oven door. You can bake these a minute less for a runnier soufflé, or more for a firm one. Remove and immediately dust with confectioners' sugar, serving soon after with the cream.

Coffee Cheesecake

FOR THE CRUST

About 9 (130 g) graham crackers

1 tablespoon coffee beans

A pinch of salt

¼ cup + 1 teaspoon (60 g) unsalted butter, melted

FOR THE FILLING

2 cups (450 g) cream cheese

⅔ cup (150 g) light brown sugar

3 large eggs

1 teaspoon vanilla extract

2 tablespoons brewed coffee, cooled

1 cup (240 g) crème fraîche

FOR THE GANACHE

⅔ cup (115 g) finely chopped dark chocolate

½ cup + 2 tablespoons (150 ml) heavy cream

The crushed coffee beans give this cheesecake character, anchoring the filling to the base like a fine layer of soil. And though it does confront, the bitterness is not dominant. The flavor of the cake is warm, dulcet, and round, not smeared with too much of any one thing.

/ *Serves 8* /

Adjust a rack to the middle of the oven, then preheat it to 350°F (180°). Grease and line an 8-inch (20-cm) round springform cake pan with parchment paper, covering the outside in a few layers of aluminum foil. Bring a kettle of water to a boil.

To make the crust, blitz the graham crackers, coffee beans, and salt to a fine crumb in a food processor. Tip into a small bowl, then stir in the butter until evenly moistened. Transfer to the prepared pan, and, with the back of a spoon, compact the crumbs into a flat layer. Bake for 10 to 12 minutes, until golden brown. Cool on a wire rack while you make the filling.

Lower the oven temperature to 250°F (120°C). Fill a deep roasting dish with a few inches of the boiling water and set it on the oven floor.

In the bowl of a stand mixer that's fitted with the paddle attachment, beat the cream cheese on medium speed for a minute or so until smooth and malleable. Pause to scrape down the bowl, then add the light brown sugar. Beat on medium speed until creamy and pale caramel in color, about 3 minutes. Again, pause to scrape, then beat in the eggs, one at a time, incorporating well after each addition. Beat in the vanilla, followed by the coffee. Lower the mixer speed and beat in the crème fraîche. Pass the batter through a fine-mesh sieve into the crust, using a rubber spatula to smooth out any lumps.

Bake for 1¼ hours, or until just set but still with a slight tremble in the middle. Turn off the oven and remove the dish of water. Let the cheesecake remain inside with the door propped open until it reaches room temperature, then refrigerate until completely cold.

To make the ganache, put the chocolate into a small heatproof bowl. Bring the cream to a simmer over medium heat, then stream it all over the chocolate. Stand for a minute, then stir slowly until smooth. Scrape the ganache over the cheesecake, smoothing it out to the edges with an offset palette knife. Return to the refrigerator and chill until set.

When you're ready to serve, unmold the cake, carefully, onto a plate. Slice with a warm knife for cleaner cuts. It will keep, loosely covered, in the refrigerator for about 3 days.

Crystallized Cocoa Nib Brownies

I liken these brownies to something of a fable. They taste that way, and how they came to be is mystical too. It's down to the elusive crackled crust that's composed of dark, crystallized cocoa nibs. I've taken inspiration here from my time in Paris, as I have most wicked things. *Folie*, or madness, is the theme, and I give credit to À la Mère de Famille and the shop's windows full of beguiled sweets. These brownies are made in a similar fashion to theirs, brooding and rich, with little reprieve of lightness.

/ ***Makes 16 brownies*** /

FOR THE CRYSTALLIZED COCOA NIBS

¼ cup (50 g) granulated sugar

⅓ cup + 1 tablespoon (50 g) cocoa nibs

½ cup (85 g) chopped dark chocolate

1 tablespoon Dutch processed cocoa powder mixed with 1 teaspoon coffee powder, for dusting

FOR THE BROWNIES

¾ cup (95 g) all-purpose flour

¾ cup + 2 tablespoons (75 g) Dutch processed cocoa powder

½ teaspoon salt

1 cup (170 g) finely chopped dark chocolate

¾ cup + 2 teaspoons (180 g) unsalted butter, cubed

1½ cups (300 g) granulated sugar

3 large eggs, cold

1 tablespoon vanilla extract

LINE a baking sheet with parchment paper.

To make the crystallized cocoa nibs, stir the sugar and 2 tablespoons water together in a small saucepan. Bring to a boil over medium-high heat and continue to cook until the syrup reaches 234°F (112°C) on a candy thermometer, about 3 minutes. Slide off the heat and tip in the nibs. Working fast with a wooden spoon, stir vigorously until the sugar has hardened into a crystallized white shell around their bodies. Scrape onto the sheet and cool.

In a medium heatproof bowl that's set over a saucepan filled with a few inches of barely simmering water, melt down the chocolate. Remove, then tip in the crystallized nibs, stirring to combine. Scrape back onto the sheet and spread the dark mass apart. Leave to set, then dust with the cocoa and coffee mixture to coat. Roughly chop, reserving half for the brownies and the rest for another use.

Adjust a rack to the middle of the oven, then preheat it to 350°F (180°C). Grease and line an 8-inch (20-cm) square baking pan with parchment paper, leaving a slight sling over the sides.

In a medium mixing bowl, whisk together the flour, cocoa, and salt.

Place the chocolate into a medium heatproof bowl and put the butter in a saucepan. Heat over medium-high heat, stirring often, until melted. Raise the heat and continue to cook, swirling often but without stirring, until a nutty brown liquid has formed. It will foam, hiss, and crackle, but subside as it nears done. Pour over the chocolate, scraping in any burnt bits that have formed. Stir slowly until melted, then set aside.

Next, in the bowl of a stand mixer that's fitted with the whisk attachment, whisk the sugar, eggs, and vanilla on medium-high speed until pale and thick, 3 to 5 minutes. Lower the speed and stream in the melted chocolate mixture. Whisk until combined, then tip in the dry ingredients.

Whisk for a further minute, or until a glossy batter has formed. Scrape into the prepared pan and smooth the edges with an offset palette knife. Stud over the crystallized nibs.

Bake for 30 minutes, or until puffed and shiny and the edges are set. The middle should still retain a slight squidge. Cool in the pan, then carefully lift the slab out. Slice the brownie into rows, then squares, the size tailored to your tolerance—I think 16 is generous—they're rich. These are best eaten on the day of making, as they'll firm with time, but can be stored in an airtight container at room temperature for 3 days.

Roasted Buckwheat Sablés

½ cup (75 g) buckwheat

1⅓ cups + 1 tablespoon (175 g) all-purpose flour

½ teaspoon salt

1 cup (230 g) salted cultured butter, like Demi-Sel, softened at room temperature

¾ cup (150 g) granulated sugar

½ cup (60 g) cocoa nibs

1 egg white, lightly beaten

the sixth sense

Switching out the nibs for flecks of dark chocolate will soften the embittered taste of these biscuits, but without extinguishing it entirely.

Sablé refers to sand or its fine texture, similar to the disintegration that occurs on the tongue when you eat one of these biscuits. They're short but not sweet, and their taste is tempestuous thanks to the buckwheat. But the final proclamation of flavor lies in the butter—a slightly salted European kind is called for.

/ ***Makes 15 biscuits*** /

Preheat the oven to 350°F (180°C). Line two baking sheets with parchment paper. Scatter the buckwheat into an even layer across one of the sheets. Roast for 8 minutes, or until nutty fragrant. Cool, then blitz to a meal in a food processor. Tip into a medium bowl and whisk in the flour and salt.

In the bowl of a stand mixer that's fitted with the paddle attachment, or using handheld electric beaters, beat the butter and ½ cup (100 g) of the sugar on medium speed until creamy, about 3 minutes. Pause to scrape down the bowl, then tip in the dry ingredients. Beat on low speed just until clumpy and soft, then beat in the cocoa nibs. Scrape the dough onto a sheet of plastic wrap and, with your hands, shape it into a taut log that's about 2 inches (5 cm) thick. Wrap, then chill until firm enough to slice, about an hour.

Adjust racks to the top and bottom thirds of the oven, then preheat it to 325°F (160°C).

To coat, scatter the remaining ¼ cup (50 g) sugar over a cutting board. Unwrap the chilled dough and, with a pastry brush, wash it thinly with egg white. Roll in the sugar, using some pressure to tack and stick the granules to the skin of the dough. Slice it into ½-inch (1.3-cm) thick rounds, then divide between the prepared sheets. Leave a few inches of space apart for spreading.

Bake for 14 to 16 minutes, rotating halfway through, until light golden. Remove and let the sablés sit on the sheets for a few minutes, then tenderly transfer them off and onto a wire rack to cool completely before serving. They're best eaten on the day of making, and will become more tender with time. Store in an airtight container at room temperature for 3 to 5 days.

Bonet

FOR THE SAUCE

1 cup (200 g) granulated sugar

FOR THE CUSTARD

1¼ cups (150 g) amaretti biscuits

1⅔ cups (400 ml) whole milk

⅔ cup (160 ml) heavy cream

⅓ cup + 1 teaspoon (60 g) finely chopped dark chocolate

¼ cup (20 g) Dutch processed cocoa powder

1 teaspoon coffee powder

4 large eggs

⅓ cup + 1 teaspoon (70 g) granulated sugar

3 tablespoons dark rum

Bonet is a traditional Piedmontese dessert, reminiscent of crème caramel in its custard-like composition but worlds apart in terms of taste. It's bitter, made with the best sorts—chocolate, coffee, and rum, as well as amaretti. But the real intensity rests in the burnt toffee sauce that sheaths the top. However far you push the scorch, from light to dark, will have a profound impact. Proceed without restraint, without caution.

/ *Serves 6 to 8* /

Preheat the oven to 300°F (150°C). Set an 8 x 4-inch (21 x 11-cm) loaf tin that holds 4 cups (1 L) into a deep roasting dish. Bring a kettle of water to a boil.

To make the sauce, put the sugar and ½ cup (120 ml) water into a medium saucepan. Bring to a boil over medium-high heat, stirring often to dissolve the granules. Raise the heat to high and continue to cook, swirling the pan occasionally but without stirring, until a dark toffee has formed. Immediately pour it into the base of the tin. Leave to harden.

To make the custard, blitz the amaretti to a sawdust-like crumb in a food processor, then set aside.

In a large saucepan, bring the milk and cream to a simmer over medium-low heat. Add the chocolate, cocoa, and coffee powder. Whisk until dissolved, then remove from the heat. In a large heatproof bowl, whisk together the eggs and sugar. Slowly stream in the warm milk mixture, whisking until combined. Whisk in the rum. Skim off any froth from the top, then stir in the amaretti. Pour into the prepared tin, then pour enough boiling water into the dish so that it reaches halfway up the sides. Tent with aluminum foil.

Bake for 1 to 1¼ hours. The bonet should feel set when lightly pressed but with a wobble to it. Remove from the water bath and cool to room temperature. Chill in the refrigerator for at least 6 hours or, preferably, overnight.

When you're ready to serve, run a warm knife around the edges to help release the custard. Invert onto a rimmed plate—the sauce should spill everywhere. Serve soon after. This will keep, loosely covered in the refrigerator, for about 1 day.

Bittersweet Chocolate Cake

FOR THE CAKE

1⅔ cups + 1 tablespoon (215 g) all-purpose flour

¾ cup + 2 tablespoons (75 g) Dutch processed cocoa powder

2 teaspoons baking soda

1 teaspoon baking powder

¼ teaspoon salt

2 cups (400 g) granulated sugar

1 cup (240 g) sour cream

½ cup + 2 teaspoons (120 ml) vegetable oil

3 large eggs

1 teaspoon vanilla extract

1 cup (240 ml) hot coffee

FOR THE SOAK

½ cup (100 g) sugar

2 tablespoons fernet, optional

FOR THE BUTTERCREAM

¾ cup (130 g) chopped dark chocolate

About 6 (180 g) large egg whites

1 cup + 2 teaspoons (210 g) granulated sugar

1½ cups + 1 teaspoon (350 g) unsalted butter, softened at room temperature

There is nostalgia that comes with a slice of chocolate cake—you can taste it. It's the birthday cake or the anniversary one. The kind that's anguished, longed, and labored over, in celebration or not, meant to demonstrate our connection through ritual, sentiment, and taste. Which also means—it must hold space for the bittersweet.

/ *Serves 8 to 12* /

Adjust a rack to the middle of the oven, then preheat it to 350°F (180°C). Grease and line three 7-inch (18-cm) cake pans with parchment paper.

Sift the flour, cocoa powder, baking soda, baking powder, and salt into a large mixing bowl, then stir in the sugar. Make a well in the center. In a separate bowl, whisk together the sour cream, oil, eggs, and vanilla. Add to the dry ingredients and whisk until the batter is thick and smooth, then slowly stream in the coffee, whisking until uniform. Divide among the prepared pans.

Bake for 30 to 35 minutes, until a skewer inserted into the middle of the cakes comes out clean and the tops spring back when lightly pressed. Cool in the pans for 15 minutes, then turn out and onto a wire rack to cool completely.

Meanwhile, make the soak. Put the sugar and ⅓ cup (80 ml) water into a small saucepan. Bring to a boil over medium heat, then remove and stir in the fernet, if using. Level off the domed cake tops with a sharp serrated knife, then brush with the soak.

To make the buttercream, put the chocolate into a medium heatproof bowl that's set over a saucepan filled with a few inches of barely simmering water. Do not let the base of the bowl touch the water below. Stir slowly over medium-low heat until melted. Set aside.

Next, put the egg whites and sugar into the bowl of a stand mixer that's fitted with the whisk attachment. Set it over the same saucepan that's still filled with water. Heat, whisking often to prevent it from catching, until it reaches 160°F (71°C) on a thermometer. The sugar granules will have dissolved and the mixture will be sticky-hot to the touch. Set onto the mixer and fit with the whisk attachment. Whisk on medium-high speed until a thick and glossy meringue has formed, about 7 minutes. Switch out the whisk for the paddle, then set the

(cont.)

speed to medium. Beat in the butter, a tablespoon at a time, until all is incorporated. Continue to beat to form a silky buttercream, then beat in the melted chocolate until mousse-like.

To assemble, set a cake layer onto a serving plate, cut side facing up. Spread over a few tablespoons of buttercream, smoothing it almost to the edges with an offset palette knife. Press on the next layer, cut side facing down. Coat again with buttercream, then add the final layer. Cover entirely with the remaining buttercream in swoops, swirls, and flourishes. Chill until set, about half an hour, before serving. Once cut, the cake should be loosely covered and kept in the refrigerator, where it'll last for 3 to 5 days. Allow time for slices to return to room temperature before eating.

Wine Pears

- 2½ cups (600 ml) full-bodied red wine
- 2 tablespoons balsamic vinegar
- Juice from ½ a lemon
- 1½ cups (300 g) granulated sugar
- 2 star anise
- A thick strip of lemon peel
- 1 vanilla bean
- 4 medium pears, like Beurré Bosc, D'Anjou, or Comice

Like a waltz, this recipe is equal parts give and take. It requires little by way of effort, and lots in terms of time. The pears should idle in the liquid and soften slowly. The result is tender stained fruit, penetrated the deepest shade of crimson straight through to the core. You could do more to them, like ice cream for serving, which leads to a mouthful that's sweet yet stung. But there's something special about capturing their essence as is—eaten in the syrup, simple and warm.

/ ***Serves 4*** /

Combine the wine, vinegar, lemon juice, sugar, and 2 cups (480 ml) water in a stockpot. Toss in the star anise and peel, then, with the tip of a sharp knife, slit open the vanilla bean. Scrape out the seeds and add them in, along with the pod. Bring to a simmer over medium heat.

Meanwhile, peel the pears, keeping their cores and stems intact. Submerge into the liquid, slightly lessening the heat. Cut out a cartouche lid from a sheet of parchment paper, then place it inside the pot. Lightly press it onto the surface to adhere.

Poach for 1¼ to 1½ hours, depending on the size of your pears. They should be tender to the point where a spoon can slip in without resistance and the wine is stained into the flesh. Discard the cartouche and remove the fruit with a slotted spoon into a bowl.

Serve warm, or cold to lessen the threat. Store any leftovers in the refrigerator for 2 to 3 days, but a little longer if resting in the residual syrup.

the sixth sense

To deepen the syrup into caramel, once the pears have been removed, raise the heat to medium-high and continue to cook until the liquid has reduced by over half to a shellacked syrup. Time isn't precise, so you'll want to keep your eye on it. It shouldn't be so thick that it sticks like molasses, but resistant enough to hold a trail. It will further set as it cools. Spoon over the pears.

Sanguinaccio

FOR THE WINE REDUCTION

1 cup (240 ml) Sangiovese

FOR THE MERINGUE

3 large egg whites

A pinch of salt

1 cup (200 g) granulated sugar

¼ cup (60 ml) wine reduction

¼ teaspoon Tasmanian pepperberries or black peppercorns, finely ground

FOR THE SALAMI

2 cups (340 g) chopped dark chocolate

½ cup + 1 tablespoon (130 g) unsalted butter, softened at room temperature

¾ cup (150 g) granulated sugar

2 tablespoons light brown sugar

4 large eggs

⅓ cup (25 g) Dutch processed cocoa powder

2 tablespoons wine reduction

½ cup (85 g) dried sour cherries, chopped

½ cup (70 g) roasted nuts, almonds, hazelnuts, or pistachios, chopped

½ cup (45 g) amaretti biscuits, roughly crushed

Confectioners' sugar, for coating

The metallic tinge in this sausage-like Italian dessert is replicated with Sangiovese instead of traditional pig's blood—a delicacy, but one that's a lot more palatable to the mind. The rich chocolate base is further strengthened with pieces of red wine meringue, a recipe that I wrote under the winter solstice, and it tastes like how it was back then too—dark, enigmatic, intense, a complete descent. The shell is hard to crack, but the inside is soft and sweet. Truss it up like a saucisson or salami, all the *s* words.

/ ***Makes a lot*** /

START the wine reduction. Put the Sangiovese into a medium saucepan and bring it to a boil over gentle heat. Lower to a simmer, then let it cook out until reduced by half, 15 minutes or so. Remove and cool.

Adjust racks to the top and bottom thirds of the oven, then preheat it to 300°F (150°C). Line two baking sheets with parchment paper.

To make the meringue, put the egg whites and salt into the bowl of a stand mixer that's fitted with the whisk attachment. Whisk on medium speed until foamy. Add the sugar, scattering it in a little at a time so as not to flood the mixture. Whisk until thick and glossy, then stream in the wine reduction. Raise the speed slightly and continue to whisk until the meringue is silky and voluminous. Whisk in the pepperberries. Dollop it into four imperfect mounds onto the prepared sheets, smoothing and swirling them out with the back of a spoon.

Bake for 1¼ to 1½ hours, until hollow and crisp to the touch. Turn off the oven and allow the meringues to cool inside until they have come to room temperature. Roughly chop, reserving 2 cups (40 g) for the salami, and the rest aside for another use.

Put the chocolate into a medium heatproof bowl, then suspend it over a saucepan that's filled with a few inches of barely simmering water. Melt over medium-low heat, then remove and cool.

Meanwhile, in the bowl of a stand mixer that's fitted with the paddle attachment, beat the butter and sugars on medium speed until pale and creamy, about 3 minutes. Pause to scrape down the bowl, then beat in the eggs one at a time, incorporating well after each addition. Lower the speed, then beat in the cocoa, followed by the wine reduction. Beat in the chocolate until silky smooth. Mix in the cherries, nuts, amaretti, and meringue pieces.

Overlap a few sheets of plastic wrap onto a work surface, then scrape on the sticky mixture. With your hands, shape it into a log that's about

14 inches (35 cm) in length and 2½ inches (6 cm) thick, using the plastic to help shape, roll, and tautly form it. Wrap, and refrigerate for a few hours until firm enough to handle.

Unwrap the log, then dust it with confectioners' sugar, thoroughly rubbing it on to coat. Truss it up with twine, like a salami.

Serve cold or close to it, slices cut with a sharp serrated knife to keep the insides intact. Store in the refrigerator, tightly wrapped, to eat within a week.

Anti-Love Cake

FOR THE CAKE

¼ cup (35 g) walnuts

3 cardamom pods

3¾ cups (360 g) almond meal

2 cups (400 g) granulated sugar

½ teaspoon ground cinnamon

½ teaspoon ground ginger

¼ teaspoon ground nutmeg

Zest from ½ a lemon

¼ teaspoon salt

⅔ cup (150 g) unsalted butter, cubed and softened at room temperature

2 large eggs, lightly beaten

1 cup + 2 tablespoons (270 g) plain yogurt

⅓ cup (45 g) mixed nuts, like pistachios, walnuts, hazelnuts, and almonds, chopped

FOR THE SYRUP

½ cup (100 g) sugar

Juice from ½ a lemon

A dash of Angostura bitters

the sixth sense

To take this back to love, drench the cake in a syrup imbued with heady rose water instead of bitters. Decorate with a sole petal.

The origins of a Persian love cake are blurred. A woman falls in love with a prince, and that love is not reciprocated, so she puts all of herself into creation with the hope of changing his mind. There isn't a resolved ending, and like any good tale, there's myth behind it. But it's meant to be amorous. Mine is true to the original, but made with a heart that's bitter.

This cake will need time to rest, best eaten soft and tender. In that silence, I think nothing of far-off storms. Instead, I start to see love in new light, now that I am not standing in its way, but its shadow.

/ *Serves 8* /

Adjust a rack to the middle of the oven, then preheat it to 350°F (180°C). Grease and line an 8-inch (20-cm) round cake pan with parchment paper.

To make the cake, put the walnuts into a dry skillet that's set over medium heat. Toast, agitating often, until dark and fragrant. Tip out and cool. Crack open the cardamom pods and extract the seeds, pulverizing them in a spice grinder with the toasted walnuts to form a meal. Transfer into a large bowl, then add the almond meal, sugar, cinnamon, ginger, nutmeg, zest, and salt. Toss in the butter. With your fingertips, rub the mixture together until evenly moistened clumps have formed. Tip a third into the prepared pan, patting it down to form a flat base.

Add the eggs and yogurt to the remaining mixture. Beat with a wooden spoon to create a homogenous batter, working out as many clumps as possible. Smooth over the base, then scatter with the mixed nuts.

Bake for 1¼ hours, or until golden brown. Tent the top with aluminum foil toward the end of baking if it starts to darken too concernedly. A skewer won't come out clean, but with a few sticky and moist crumbs attached. Transfer the cake to a wire rack.

While it cools, make the syrup. Bring the sugar, lemon juice, and ¼ cup (60 ml) water to a simmer over medium heat in a small saucepan. Remove, then stir in the bitters. Drench the cake. Leave to stand for 15 minutes, then unmold, tentatively—it'll be fragile.

Serve at room temperature, or close to it. It's wonderful with tangy yogurt on the side. This is best eaten on the day of making, but will keep in an airtight container for 1 day, or up to 3 in the refrigerator.

Sweet

Sugar is sweet on the surface, but it's not always. It is what we make of it, and what we make is dessert. The last course cannot exist without sweetness. It signifies closure, a coming to an end in the best possible way. It's how I recall the moments of my life; those that have come before—who fed me and then who fed them. How with time, even sweetness can heal a lineage. ¶ The women in my family know what it means to endure, and because of that, our palates are the same—sweet. "Too much sugar can be a sickness too, Thalia," once, I was told. But I was led by example. My great-grandmother would lick golden syrup straight off the lid of the tin, that sticky substance her personal gold. I like it similar, as does my grandmother. She swirls sugar into everything and "improves" red wine with lemonade. She doesn't know it, but she is tempering the bitter, and I let her, because I also know she's seen enough of it. The hour of darkness she inherited had stretched out into a life, and when I opened my eyes, I realized, it was mine. ¶ Armed with their guidance, in the kitchen and out, I carry with me their sacrifice, which I also think is their sweetness, and then I work to transform it into something more palatable. In that light, sugar becomes the fix. Or at least the path toward it. ¶ Sweetness makes us weak, it makes us strong, and the recipes contained within this chapter unite that polarity. They're nostalgic, familiar yet foreign, with sugar as the star. But there are ways to sweeten that aren't just reliant on use of the granule—other deep wells, spurting from ingredient as well as memory, I find alluring, and treatments, like burning into caramel, which seem like an antithesis but really make flavor greater, without also becoming "too sweet." During these acts, I learn to anticipate need, and feed the narrative, and appetite, I want. It's through dessert that I can return to the past, no longer in the same form, but nonetheless soothed. ¶ A recipe handed down is not stagnant—it moves.

Paris-Brest

The complexities of the patisserie darling Paris-Brest can make it seem graceless, and that's the point. This is not something you want to force into submission—I've tried and it doesn't work. Best to let it end how it needs to.

To streamline the process, some of the components can be made in advance—the choux the evening before, the crème pâtissière the morning of. But the mousseline should be finished before assembly. It's temperamental, and not just because of the burnt sugar.

/ *Serves 8* /

FOR THE PÂTE À CHOUX

¼ cup (60 ml) whole milk

¼ cup + ½ teaspoon (60 g) unsalted butter, cubed

¼ teaspoon salt

⅔ cup + 1 teaspoon (85 g) all-purpose flour, sifted

2 large eggs

1 large egg, whisked with 1 teaspoon whole milk, for the wash

A handful of flaked almonds, for the top

FOR THE CRÈME PÂTISSIÈRE

1¼ cups (300 ml) heavy cream

1 cup + 3 tablespoons (285 ml) whole milk

¾ cup (150 g) sugar

4 large egg yolks

¼ cup (32 g) cornstarch

FOR THE MOUSSELINE

1 cup (2 sticks/230 g) unsalted butter, softened at room temperature

1 teaspoon vanilla bean paste

A pinch of salt

Confectioners' sugar, for finishing

Position a rack to the middle of the oven, then preheat it to 375°F (190°C).

Using an 8-inch (20-cm) cake ring as a guide, stencil a circle onto a piece of parchment paper. Place it onto a baking sheet, marked side facing down. Fit a pastry bag with a ½-inch (1.3-cm) round tip, then set the bag into a cocktail shaker or tall glass, which will help hold the weight when you go to fill it.

To make the pâte à choux, put the milk, butter, salt, and ¼ cup (60 ml) water into a wide saucepan that's set over medium-high heat. With a wooden spoon, stir as the butter melts. Bring to a boil, then slide off the heat and tip in the flour. Work vigorously to incorporate and smooth out any lumps. Return to the heat and keep stirring for a few more minutes, until the dough balls together. A thin film will have lined the base of the pan. Scrape into the bowl of a stand mixer and fit on the paddle attachment. Beat on medium speed until all of the steam has escaped. Beat in the eggs, one at a time, waiting to fully blend before adding in the next. The mixture will split at first, then pull into a velvety paste. Scrape into the pastry bag and snip off the tip.

There will be some resistance when piping out the dough, so smear a little of it on the underside of the paper to help stick it down. Holding the bag at an angle, and with consistent pressure, pipe a ring along your traced circle. Pipe a second ring along the outside of the first, so that they are touching. Pipe a third ring on top, nestling it in between the groove where the two below meet. Brush lightly with egg wash and sprinkle with the almonds.

(cont.)

Bake for 35 minutes. You'll want to rely on time instead of visual cues to check for doneness here, as opening the door during baking will cause steam to escape and the pastry to deflate. The choux will be golden brown, crisp, and hollow when done. Turn off the oven and pry open the door, leaving the ring to cool in the residual heat.

To make the crème pâtissière, bring the cream and milk to a simmer in a medium saucepan that's set over gentle heat. In a separate saucepan, stir together ½ cup (100 g) of the sugar and 2 tablespoons water. Let it cook untouched over medium-high heat until a thin and deeply caramelized liquid has formed. Meanwhile, whisk together the remaining ¼ cup (50 g) sugar, the yolks, and cornstarch in a separate heatproof bowl. As soon as the sugar has tainted, slowly stream in the cream and milk, whisking carefully to combine. It will sputter, seize, and resist at first, then dissolve. Lower the heat. Ladle a little into the yolks, whisking to acclimatize and combine. Pour it all back into the pan that's set on the stove. Continue to heat, whisking constantly, until smooth, thick, and glossy, like custard. Pass through a fine-mesh sieve into a medium heatproof bowl, then cover the surface with plastic wrap. Cool to room temperature before use.

When you're almost ready to serve, make the mousseline. In the bowl of a stand mixer that's fitted with the paddle attachment, beat the butter on medium speed for a minute or so until smooth and malleable. Beat in a tablespoon of the crème pâtissière at a time, waiting until blended before adding in the next. Scrape down the bowl as needed to ensure even incorporation. Beat in the vanilla and salt, then switch out the paddle for the whisk attachment. Whisk for a few minutes on high speed until silky, thick, and aerated. If at any point your mousseline starts to split, it usually has to do with the integration of two mixtures at disparate temperatures. It can be salvaged. Transfer a quarter of it into a saucepan and heat until almost melted. Whisk back into the mousseline until emulsified. Transfer to a pastry bag that's fitted with a ¾-inch (2-cm) open star tip.

Set the choux ring onto a plate. With a sharp serrated knife, slice it horizontally, so that you have two halves. On the bottom half, pipe out swirls of the mousseline to cover, then lightly press on the top. Dust with confectioners' sugar before serving.

This is best eaten on the day of making, as it will soften with time. Store leftovers in an airtight container in the refrigerator for up to 3 days.

the sixth sense

Paris-Brest is work and reward. To further indulge, pair with Champagne, which is hedonistic yet complementary, with its rich, yeasted, buttery effervescence. This is a celebratory dessert you want to end with. Pair with a lustrous bottle.

Rings of Time Cookies

2 cups (250 g) all-purpose flour

½ teaspoon baking soda

1 teaspoon salt

1 cup (2 sticks/230 g) unsalted butter, cubed

1¼ cups (250 g) granulated sugar

½ cup (110 g) dark brown sugar

1 large egg

1 tablespoon toasted sesame oil

1 teaspoon vanilla extract

¾ cup (130 g) finely chopped dark chocolate

2 tablespoons roasted sesame seeds

Flaky sea salt, for finishing

Cookies, naturally, are a sweet thing. These are molassic and dark, with a good amount of roasted sesame seeds to interrupt the predicted path. They should warp—allow nature to take its course. Like rings of a tree trunk, these chart the time and tempests of taste.

/ *Makes 15 cookies* /

In a medium mixing bowl, whisk together the flour, baking soda, and salt.

Put the butter into a saucepan that's set over medium heat. Stir until melted, then pour it into a large bowl. Add the sugars and whisk until combined. Whisk in the egg, oil, and vanilla until glossy. Tip in the dry ingredients. Stir with a wooden spoon to form a soft and sticky dough, then mix in the chocolate and seeds until evenly distributed. Cover and chill in the refrigerator until just firm enough to handle, about half an hour.

Meanwhile, adjust racks to the top, middle, and bottom thirds of the oven. Preheat it to 350°F (180°C). Line three baking sheets with parchment paper.

Portion the dough into mounds that are about 2½ ounces (70 g) in weight, or about 2 heaping tablespoons. Roll into balls with your hands, then divide them among the prepared sheets. They'll spread during baking, so leave enough space. I fit 4 per sheet, setting the rest aside to be baked off later.

Bake for 10 to 12 minutes, rotating halfway, until thin, rippled, and golden, the edges crisped. Let the cookies cool on the sheets for a few minutes, before transferring off with an offset palette knife onto a wire rack to cool further. Finish lightly with flaky salt before serving. They'll keep, stored in an airtight container, at room temperature for about 3 days.

Caramelized White Chocolate

This is a labor of love. To witness the process of caramelized white chocolate is to witness the art of transformation. At first there is resistance, then with work and yielding, something of greater character can develop. The aim is to simulate the subtle scorching of sugar, milk, and fat, using low heat and agitation. It takes an ingredient that is often considered sickly and fills it with potential. Push it to gold or keep it blonde, the choice is yours, but the chocolate used matters. The higher the cocoa butter percentage, the more pliant it is to melting.

/ *About 2 cups* /

2 cups (340 g) finely chopped white chocolate

Flaky sea salt, to finish

Adjust a rack to the middle of the oven, then preheat it to 275°F (135°C).

Scatter the white chocolate into an even layer across a rimmed baking dish. Roast for 10 minutes. Immediately remove the dish, then, with a rubber spatula, smooth out the chocolate. It may seem resistant at first, but will liquefy with consistency, handling, and time. Wipe in the sticky-excess from the spatula, then return to the oven. Roast for another 5 to 7 minutes. Continue this process of roasting, removing, smoothing, and then returning to the oven until the white chocolate has taken on a caramelized tone. It can take up to an hour, depending on your depth preference. Season with flaky salt.

Use as desired or transfer to a jar, allowing to cool completely before sealing. It will keep for a few weeks. If required, submerge in barely simmering water to melt the chocolate back into a workable consistency or, simply, to eat.

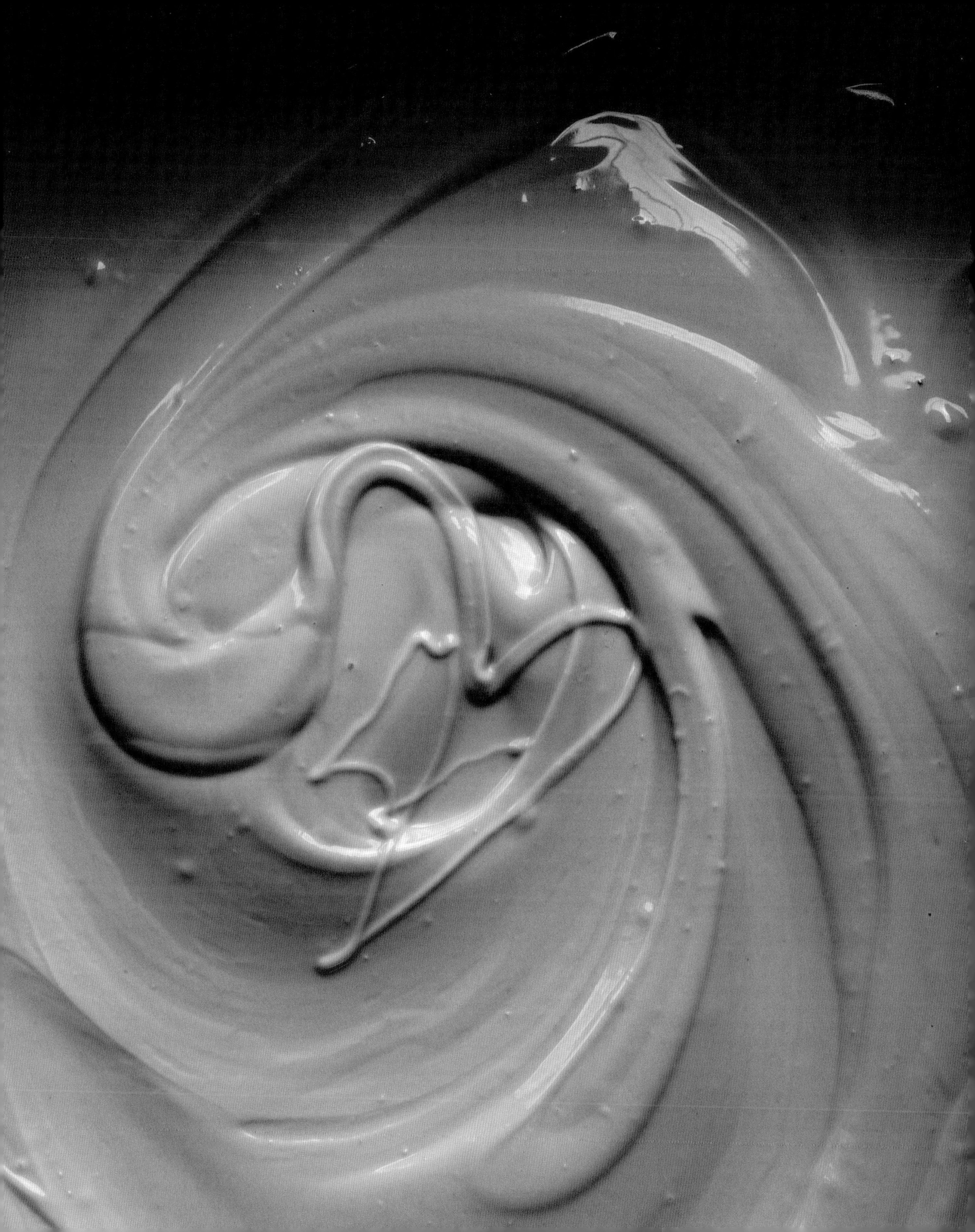

Pineapple Upside-Down Cake

Despite its initial tartness, a ripe pineapple has the propensity to turn deliciously sweet when caramelized, and there's no way better, I think, to highlight the fruit than in an upside-down cake. It's exceptionally tender and moist, with a desirable sting that's softened out by a blend of spices. Eat slightly warm, for its best.

/ *Serves 8* /

FOR THE PINEAPPLE

⅓ cup (75 g) unsalted butter, cubed

½ cup (110 g) light brown sugar

¼ teaspoon ground turmeric

A pinch of ground cloves, cardamom, and ginger

1 star anise

Juice from ½ a small lime

1 tablespoon dark rum

1 medium pineapple (580 g weight of flesh), peeled, cored, and cut lengthwise into ¼-inch (.6-cm) thick slices

FOR THE CAKE

2¼ cups (280 g) all-purpose flour

1¼ teaspoons baking powder

½ teaspoon baking soda

¼ teaspoon salt

¾ cup + 1 tablespoon (185 g) unsalted butter, softened at room temperature

1¼ cups (250 g) granulated sugar

3 large eggs

1 teaspoon vanilla extract

1 cup (240 ml) crème fraîche

Adjust a rack to the middle of the oven, then preheat it to 350°F (180°C). Grease and line an 8-inch (20-cm) cake pan with parchment paper.

For the pineapple, combine the butter, sugar, turmeric, cloves, cardamom, ginger, and star anise in a wide cast-iron skillet that's set over medium heat. Stir until melted, dissolved, and bubbling, then stir in the lime juice and rum, if using. Nestle in the pineapple, setting pieces aside to be caramelized afterward if they don't fit. Cook, turning occasionally, until tender. Overlap into the prepared pan and set aside while you make the cake batter.

To make the cake, sift the flour, baking powder, baking soda, and salt into a medium mixing bowl.

In the bowl of a stand mixer that's fitted with the paddle attachment, or using handheld electric beaters, beat the butter and sugar until light and fluffy, 3 to 5 minutes. Pause to scrape down the bowl, then beat in the eggs, one at a time, incorporating well after each addition. Beat in the vanilla, then lower the speed. Tip in half of the dry ingredients. Beat until just combined, then beat in the crème fraîche, followed by the last of the dry ingredients. Scrape the batter into the pan, smoothing it out over the fruit.

Bake for about an hour, until golden brown. A skewer inserted into the middle of the cake should come out with a few moist crumbs attached. Cool in the pan for 10 minutes, then invert onto a serving plate. Unmold carefully. Serve warm or close to it, gilded with crème fraîche. This cake is best eaten on the day of making.

the sixth sense

Together, pineapple and rum make perfect sense. There's some spiked here, but with heat comes a reduction of aroma, ethanol, and bite, and that's what I like about it best. Glaze a few tablespoons of good rum over the top of the cake as it cools, to enhance.

Stuffed Scones

- 1 cup (240 ml) heavy cream
- 1 large egg
- 1 teaspoon vanilla extract
- 2½ cups (315 g) all-purpose flour
- ⅔ cup (65 g) almond meal
- 1½ tablespoons baking powder
- Zest from ½ a small orange
- ¼ teaspoon salt
- ¼ cup (50 g) granulated sugar
- ¾ cup (170 g) unsalted butter, cold and cut into ½-inch (1.3-cm) cubes
- ⅓ cup + 1 tablespoon (130 g) jam or marmalade
- Heavy cream, for brushing
- Raw sugar, for sprinkling

These scones should twist, slip, and contort during baking, with the kind of surrealist shapes that even Dalí would be proud of. The jam or marmalade used will impact how they end—choose your path, bitter or sweet.

/ *Makes 6 scones* /

Adjust racks to the top and bottom thirds of the oven, then preheat it to 350°F (180°C). Line two baking sheets with parchment paper.

Lightly stir together the cream, egg, and vanilla in a small bowl or measuring cup just to combine. Keep cold until needed.

In a large mixing bowl, whisk together the flour, almond meal, baking powder, zest, and salt. Stir in the granulated sugar, then add the butter and toss it through to coat. With a pastry blender, your fingertips, or a combination of both, blend in the cubes to form damp, sandy crumbles. A few coarse chunks are fine to remain. Push the dry ingredients aside to make a well in the middle, then stream the liquid ingredients into it. Stir with a wooden spoon until rough and shaggy, then tip the mixture out and onto a floured work surface.

Using your hands, bring the dough together into a mound, incorporating as much of the dry flaky bits as possible. Pat it down until it's about 1½ inches (4 cm) thick. Fold in half, then give it a quarter turn and pat down again to re-form. Repeat three more times until the dough has made a full circular rotation. It'll be tender at first but strengthen as you fold. Shape into a ¾-inch (2-cm) rectangle. Spread over the jam or marmalade. Fold over itself, to enclose.

Cut into 6 triangle-shaped scones. Divide them between the baking sheets, leaving space for spreading and oozing. Brush lightly with cream, then sprinkle with raw sugar.

Bake for about 25 minutes, rotating halfway, until golden brown. Stand for a few minutes, until firm enough to handle, then transfer onto a wire rack to cool further.

Serve the scones warm or at room temperature. They're best eaten soon after making, but will keep, stored in an airtight container at room temperature, for 2 to 3 days. Warm slightly, for their best.

Fallen Fog Cake

Drenched in caramel, this fondant-esque fallen cake is nothing if not stormed. The flavor is taken from the infamous "London Fog," a mixture of Earl Grey tea, honey, and steamed milk, which unites in a smoggy brew to soothe the soul. It goes well with dark chocolate, which has a linear sharpness useful to diffuse the ultra-sweet. You won't need to use all of the caramel, but it's easier to make in large volume than less. Reserve half for another use or, indulgently, serve at the table.

/ *Serves 8* /

FOR THE CAKE

⅔ cup (150 g) unsalted butter, cubed

1½ cups (255 g) chopped dark chocolate

5 large eggs, separated

⅔ cup (50 g) Dutch processed cocoa powder, sifted

½ cup + 2 tablespoons (150 ml) whole milk, lightly warmed

2 tablespoons whisky

¼ teaspoon salt

⅔ cup (135 g) granulated sugar

FOR THE CARAMEL

½ teaspoon Earl Grey tea leaves

½ cup (100 g) granulated sugar

½ cup + 1 tablespoon (190 g) honey

½ cup (1 stick/115 g) unsalted butter, cubed

⅓ cup + 2 tablespoons (110 ml) heavy cream

A pinch of fleur de sel

ADJUST a rack to the middle of the oven, then preheat it to 350°F (180°C). Grease and line an 8-inch (20-cm) round springform cake pan with parchment paper.

To make the cake, melt the butter and chocolate together in a large heatproof bowl that's set over a saucepan filled with a few inches of barely simmering water. Do not let the base of the bowl touch the water below. Remove and whisk in the egg yolks, cocoa powder, milk, whisky, and salt.

Next, in the bowl of a stand mixer that's fitted with the whisk attachment, whisk the egg whites on medium speed until foamy. Scatter in the sugar, a tablespoon at a time, until it's all used up. Continue to whisk until a thick and glossy meringue has formed. Fold a third into the chocolate mixture to loosen, then another third, followed by the last, becoming gentler each time to retain as much air as possible. Scrape into the prepared pan.

Bake for 30 to 35 minutes, until cracked and just set. Transfer to a wire rack and leave to fall in the pan completely.

To make the caramel, blitz the tea and sugar in a spice grinder until fine. Alternatively, you can use a mortar and pestle, pummeling with force to achieve a similar consistency. Add into a saucepan, along with the honey. Cook over medium-high heat, swirling the pan often but without stirring, until bubbling, fragrant, and deep amber in hue. Slide off from the heat and whisk in the butter, cream, and fleur de sel, being careful, as it will steam and spit. Slide back onto the heat and return to a boil, then transfer into a medium heatproof bowl. Leave to cool and thicken on the kitchen counter, stirring occasionally, then pour half of the caramel over the cake. Let it sink in.

Slice and serve once settled. The cake will keep, covered, in the refrigerator for 3 to 5 days, during which time it will meld, intensify, and squidge, like a brownie.

the sixth sense

Caramel is sweet, even more so when made with honey. To quickly shift this from sweet to bitter, replace the sauce with a ganache made of ⅔ cup (115 g) finely chopped dark chocolate and ½ cup (120 ml) heavy cream. The pouring, sinking, and settling remains the same.

Oeufs à la Neige

FOR THE CRÈME ANGLAISE

2 cups (480 ml) whole milk

1 vanilla bean

5 large egg yolks

⅓ cup (70 g) granulated sugar

2 tablespoons honey

¼ teaspoon orange blossom water

FOR THE CRÈME MERINGUES

5 large egg whites

A pinch of salt

1 cup (120 g) confectioners' sugar, sifted

FOR POACHING

4 cups (960 ml) whole milk

Freshly grated nutmeg, for the top

A good-quality honey, to finish

Flaked almonds, roasted

the sixth sense

Once I was told to treat your snow eggs like a sundae. And while that evokes all kinds of sacrilegious thoughts, I agree. How you finish it is personal and tells a tale. Roasted almonds are traditional, as is burnt sugar, which sets to a crisp with exposure to the custard. But what I value most about this dessert is the uninterrupted softness. Stewed rhubarb or quince is ideal for that.

Montparnasse, New Year's Day. Oeufs à la neige under wintered skies, all so silent and still, I can almost see clearly.

The ones I remember from my time in Paris were made with an elegant and thin anglaise that still retained just enough weight to support the clouds that float atop it. You can prepare the custard the night before, allowing time for rest, but the meringues should be poached right before serving. They're prone to weeping and lose structure with time.

/ *Serves 4* /

FIRST, make the anglaise. Pour the milk into a large saucepan. With the tip of a sharp knife, split open the vanilla bean and scrape the seeds out from along the spine, adding them into the milk, along with the emptied pod. Bring to a simmer over medium heat. Meanwhile, in a medium heatproof bowl, whisk together the egg yolks, sugar, honey, and orange blossom water.

Stream half of the hot milk into the yolks, whisking well to combine, then transfer back into the pan. Continue to gently heat, stirring slowly and constantly, until the sauce has taken on enough resistance to slick the back of a spoon. Pour into a large heatproof bowl and cover the surface with plastic wrap. Chill thoroughly.

To make the meringues, put the egg whites and salt into the bowl of a stand mixer that's fitted with the whisk attachment. Whisk on medium speed to soft peaks. Scatter in the confectioners' sugar a little at a time, being cautious not to flood the mixture. Whisk to form stiff and shiny peaks. Meanwhile, bring the milk for poaching to a simmer in a wide saucepan over low heat. Line a baking sheet with parchment paper.

With a warm dessert spoon, scoop out oval-shaped amounts from the meringue, using a second spoon to help ease it off and into the warm milk. Poach in batches until just firm, 2 to 3 minutes on each side. Remove with a slotted spoon onto the prepared sheet.

Divide the anglaise among bowls. Top with meringues, a few apiece, and finish with a pinch of nutmeg, drizzle of honey, and almonds. Eat soon after.

Meringata

FOR THE MERINGUE

1½ cups (300 g) granulated sugar

6 large egg whites

¼ teaspoon cream of tartar

¼ cup (25 g) ground almonds

FOR THE BRITTLE CHOCOLATE BITS

½ cup (85 g) chopped dark chocolate

1 tablespoon coconut oil

FOR THE FILLING

2 cups (480 ml) heavy cream

⅓ cup (40 g) confectioners' sugar, sifted

1 teaspoon vanilla extract

FOR THE SAUCE

1 cup (240 ml) heavy cream

¾ cup (130 g) finely chopped dark chocolate

2 tablespoons espresso or amaro

A glorified ice cream cake that shatters like a dream, meringata offers a sense of fragility. It's pure and sinful, light yet dark, and heals through its harmonization of opposites. Each mouthful is fleeting, and it destabilizes fast. I make the meringue layers the morning of, then assemble the cake in the early afternoon, which leaves enough time for it to freeze before dessert is demanded. The sauce should always be finished prior to serving, though, either with espresso or amaro, which, for me, signifies the end.

/ *Serves 8* /

Adjust racks to the top, middle, and lower thirds of the oven, then preheat it to 300°F (150°C). Line three baking sheets with parchment paper.

To make the meringues, scatter the sugar into an even layer over one of the prepared baking sheets. Toast until the edges of the granules are starting to tinge, about 8 minutes. Remove, then lower the temperature to 225°F (110°C).

In the bowl of a stand mixer that's fitted with the whisk attachment, whisk the egg whites and cream of tartar on medium speed until foamy. Add the sugar a little at a time, waiting until it has all been incorporated before scattering in the next. Continue to whisk to form a thick and glossy meringue. Fold in the almonds. Divide among the prepared sheets, smoothing the sticky mass out with an offset palette knife to form three circles that are about 9 inches (23 cm) in width and 1 inch (2.5 cm) in height. Slightly divot in the centers.

Bake for about an hour, until firm and dry. Turn off the oven and prop open the door, leaving the meringues inside to cool to room temperature.

Next, make the brittle chocolate bits. Put the chocolate into a medium heatproof bowl, then suspend it over a saucepan that's filled with a few inches of barely simmering water. Melt over medium-low heat, then remove and stir in the oil. Pour onto a lined baking sheet, slicking it out and into an ultra-thin layer. Freeze until solid, then fracture into shards. Store in the freezer until needed.

When you're ready to assemble, make the filling. In the bowl of a stand mixer that's fitted with the whisk attachment, whip the cream, confectioners' sugar, and vanilla to supple peaks on medium speed.

Position a meringue onto a serving plate. Spread with half of the cream all the way to the edges. Scatter with some brittle chocolate bits, reserving the largest for the top. Lay over a second meringue, lightly pressing down

the sixth sense

My time in Florence taught me many things, mostly sweet but also not. There, I liked the meringatas with rare and precious gleaming fruits, like tiny wild strawberries and raspberries, which added to the cake's ethereal nature. If the season permits, I use them here. I also make this wintered, filled with praline and an assortment of poached fruits. I let it be what it must, a vision.

to adhere. Cover with the remaining cream and more chocolate. Top with the final meringue, then pierce it with shards. Freeze the cake until firm.

For the sauce, put the cream and chocolate into a medium saucepan that's set over medium-low heat. Whisk until melted, then remove and stir in the espresso or amaro. Serve the sauce warm, spooned over thick slices of frozen meringata. Keep leftovers tightly covered in the freezer for 5 days or up to a week.

Extra-Virgin Olive Oil Cake

2 cups + 2 tablespoons (265 g) all-purpose flour

⅓ cup (30 g) almond meal

2 teaspoons baking powder

Zest and juice from 1 lemon

½ teaspoon salt

1⅓ cups (300 ml) extra-virgin olive oil

1 cup (240 ml) whole milk

4 large eggs

1¼ cups + 1 tablespoon (265 g) granulated sugar, plus more for the top

Flaked almonds, for the top

I think desserts are best when simple, though simplicity often is deceptive. This cake takes root from the many others that have come before it. It's intense, and a slice should be served alone. The flavor will change depending on the olive oil used. Grassy, fatty, astringent kinds won't work—they taint the cake's fragility. Opt for a high-grade oil with a smooth mouthfeel and refined fruitful notes, faithful to the hand or place that created it. Some slight bitterness is fine, if not ideal.

/ ***Serves 8*** /

Adjust a rack to the middle of the oven, then preheat it to 350°F (180°). Grease and line an 8-inch (20-cm) round springform cake pan with parchment paper.

Whisk together the flour, almond meal, baking powder, zest, and salt into a medium bowl. In a separate large bowl or measuring jug, stir together the oil, milk, and lemon juice.

In the bowl of a stand mixer that's fitted with the whisk attachment, or with a balloon whisk and some heavy-handed action, whisk the eggs and sugar on high speed until pale, thick, and voluminous, 3 to 5 minutes. The mixture should fall back onto itself in a trail when the whisk is lifted. Lower the speed and stream in the liquids. Whisk until combined. Whisk in the dry ingredients until almost combined—some floury streaks should remain—then, using a rubber spatula, finish folding together by hand until the batter is uniform. Pour into the prepared pan. Scatter with almonds, then with sugar.

Bake for 50 minutes to an hour, until domed, crackled, and golden. A skewer inserted into the middle should come out clean. Transfer to a wire rack and cool for 10 minutes, then unmold and leave to cool completely. Because this cake is made with oil, it will keep well for 2 to 3 days, intensifying as it sits. Store in an airtight container in a cool, dark place at room temperature.

the sixth sense

No better end than to serve a slice with another liquid gold, the eucharist, Vin Santo, an Italian dessert wine.

GIVE US THIS DAY OUR DAILY BREAD

Sugar Buns

These aren't fast to make, but the way you'll want to eat them is. Split, pried, then filled to the point of rupture, they're heavenly, every bit as pillowed as they look.

/ *Makes 9 buns* /

FOR THE CRÈME PÂTISSIÈRE

2¼ cups (540 ml) whole milk

1 vanilla bean

5 large egg yolks

⅓ cup + 2 teaspoons (75 g) granulated sugar

3 tablespoons honey

¼ cup + 1 tablespoon (40 g) cornstarch

A pinch of salt

2 tablespoons unsalted butter, softened at room temperature

FOR THE BRIOCHE

2½ cups (315 g) all-purpose flour

¼ cup (50 g) granulated sugar

2½ teaspoons (7 g) instant dried yeast

1 teaspoon lemon zest

¼ teaspoon salt

2 large eggs

½ cup (120 ml) whole milk

⅓ cup + 1 tablespoon (90 g) unsalted butter, softened at room temperature

1 egg yolk, lightly whisked with 1 tablespoon whole milk, for the wash

FOR FILLING AND FINISHING

½ cup (120 ml) heavy cream

Confectioners' sugar, for dusting

First, make the crème pâtissière. Pour the milk into a large saucepan, then split open the vanilla bean and scrape out the seeds. Add into the pan, along with the pod. Bring to a simmer over medium-low heat. Meanwhile, in a medium heatproof bowl, whisk together the egg yolks, sugar, honey, cornstarch, and salt. As soon as the milk has reached temperature, stream it into the yolks, whisking to combine. Pour it all back into the saucepan. Continue to gently heat, whisking continuously until smooth, thick, and glossy. Slide off from the heat and whisk in the butter. Pass through a fine-mesh sieve into a large heatproof bowl, then cover the surface with plastic wrap. Refrigerate until completely cold.

For the brioche, put the flour, sugar, yeast, zest, and salt into the bowl of a stand mixer that's fitted with the dough hook attachment. Mix on low speed to combine, then add the eggs and milk. Raise the speed to medium and knead for a few minutes, until the dough has gone from rough and shaggy to smooth and elastic. Add the butter a tablespoon at a time, waiting until each spoonful has been blended in before adding the next. Continue to knead until a velvety dough ball has formed around the blade.

Transfer to a greased large bowl, then cover and leave to rise in a warm spot until doubled in size, 1½ to 2 hours. Once risen, you can refrigerate the dough for several hours to slow fermentation and make it easier to handle, or proceed with shaping.

Line two baking sheets with parchment paper. Dust a work surface with flour, then scrape the dough out and onto it. Divide into equal mounds that are about 2¼ ounces (65 g) in weight. Shape each into a taut ball by cupping the dough in your hand and tenderly stretching the sides into the center in a circular rotating motion. Divide between the prepared sheets, leaving space for expansion. Cover and leave until just under doubled in size, less than an hour. The dough will be puffed and spring back when lightly pressed.

Adjust racks to the top and bottom thirds of the oven, then preheat it to 350°F (180°C).

Brush the dough with the egg wash. Bake for 15 to 17 minutes, rotating halfway through, until golden brown. Stand on the sheets for a few minutes, then transfer the buns off and onto a wire rack to cool completely before filling.

To fill, first, in the bowl of a stand mixer that's fitted with the whisk attachment, whip the cream to soft peaks on medium speed. Remove the chilled crème pâtissière and give it a good stir to loosen. Fold in the whipped cream until no streaks remain. Scrape into a pastry bag and snip an inch off the tip. With a sharp serrated knife, split the buns straight down the middle, keeping an inch from the base intact. Dust with confectioners' sugar, then bloat each with the filling. Serve soon after.

the sixth sense

The best time to eat these buns is a point of contention—soon after making, always, to ensure their freshness, but I adore them cold the next morning, when the cream has absorbed into the brioche. The size of them is generous, and, likely, there will be leftovers. I never want to keep them for too long. With that mind, I sometimes place a core of marmalade beneath the cream filling. The bitter lessens the sweet, rehydrates the crumb, and makes these good for breakfast as well as dessert.

Glazed Apple Tart

FOR THE TART

½ cup (1 stick/115 g) unsalted butter, cubed

4 large red apples

Juice from a lemon

2 sheets (about 350 g) all-butter puff pastry

¼ cup (50 g) granulated sugar

FOR THE GLAZE

½ cup + 2 tablespoons (125 g) granulated sugar

1 star anise

1 teaspoon honey

2 tablespoons Calvados, optional

This tart is deceptive. It's an Eve-like dessert; *tarte fine aux pommes* in French, but I've also heard it answer to many other names. *Facile*, or easy, are also words associated with it—which is true but also not, for beneath the layers is a latent bittersweet that will surprise.

/ *Serves 4 to 6* /

Adjust a rack to the middle of the oven, then preheat it to 425°F (220°C). Line a baking sheet with parchment paper.

For the tart, put the butter into a medium saucepan. Heat over medium-low, stirring often, until melted. Raise the heat to high and continue to cook, swirling often but without stirring, until a nutty brown liquid has formed. It will foam, hiss, and crackle, but subside as it nears done. Pour into a small heatproof bowl, scraping in any burnt bits. Set aside until needed.

Peel and core the apples, working fast and rubbing the flesh with lemon juice if needed to prevent browning. With a sharp knife or a mandoline, cut the fruit into thin slices, about ¾ inch (2 cm) thick.

Place the puff pastry onto the prepared sheet, brushing enough burnt butter between the layers to adhere. Scatter with a generous tablespoon or so of the sugar, then arrange over the apple slices, overlapping them in a linear way and leaving an inch from the edges to form a border. Slick with more burnt butter, then scatter with remaining sugar. Crimp the edges to seal.

Bake for 10 minutes, then rotate the sheet and lower the temperature to 400°F (200°C). Continue to bake for another 30 to 35 minutes, until golden brown and crisp.

Meanwhile, make the glaze. Combine the sugar, star anise, honey, and ⅓ cup (80 ml) water in a small saucepan. Bring to a boil over medium heat, then lower slightly and continue to cook down for a few more minutes, to a resistant syrup. Remove and stir in the Calvados, if using. Cool, then brush the tart generously.

Serve warm or close to it, with crème fraîche or ice cream on the side. This is best eaten on the day of making.

Honey Cake

FOR THE LAYERS

2 cups (250 g) all-purpose flour

¾ cup (90 g) buckwheat flour

½ cup + 2 tablespoons (210 g) honey

½ cup + 1 tablespoon (130 g) unsalted butter, cubed

½ cup (100 g) granulated sugar

1 teaspoon baking soda

¼ teaspoon salt

4 large eggs, cold

FOR THE SOAK

¼ cup (60 ml) whisky

FOR THE CREAM

2½ cups (600 ml) heavy cream

⅔ cup (160 g) crème fraîche

2 tablespoons granulated sugar

1 teaspoon vanilla bean paste

I associate my Russian heritage with sharp women. I remember my grandmother and her friends, sitting like disciples in the back row of our church. Their tongues as seasoned as their skin—bitter and biting. I still taste the parables on the tips of my teeth. It felt harsh, but there was also a lot of sweetness, and not just in the desserts they would share after.

Often considered a grandmother's cake, this medovik is nothing but complex and technique driven. And if the cake is anything like the women I remember, the sweet layers are hidden, revealed only to those who can handle it.

/ *Serves 8 to 10* /

Adjust racks to the top, middle, and bottom thirds of the oven, then preheat it to 350°F (180°C). Set out as many baking sheets as will fit at a time, usually three, then tear out ten sheets of parchment paper. Stencil a circle onto each, using a 7-inch (18-cm) cake ring as a guide. Flip them over so that the drawn side is face down.

To make the layers, first, sift the flours into a large bowl.

Put the honey, butter, and sugar into a large saucepan. Cook over medium heat, stirring often, until melted. Remove and whisk in the baking soda and salt. The mixture should foam, then settle, softly. Whisk in the eggs, one at a time, until evenly incorporated. Whisk in the flours. The batter should be smooth, viscous, and velvety in texture.

Put an offset palette knife into a tall glass of warm water. Portion a few tablespoons of batter into the middle of one of the stenciled circles. Dry the spatula, then use it to spread the batter into a thin and even layer across it. Slide onto the prepared sheets, leaving the rest aside to be baked off after.

Bake for 6 to 7 minutes, until golden brown. You'll want to set a timer for this, as they turn fast. Remove, and cool on the sheets for a few minutes, then lift off and onto the kitchen counter to rest while you bake off the remaining layers. You should finish with 10 in total.

Transfer two of the most disparate looking layers into a large bowl. Finely crumble them with your fingertips. Brush the whisky over the tops of the remaining layers.

Next, in the bowl of a stand mixer that's fitted with the whisk attachment, whip the cream, crème fraîche, sugar, and vanilla paste to soft and supple peaks on medium speed.

(cont.)

Set a cake layer onto a serving plate. Spoon about 3 tablespoons of the whipped cream over the top, smoothing it all the way to the edges. It's fine, if not helpful, if it spills over a little. Rest a second layer over the top, pressing it down lightly. Again, spread with cream. Repeat this process to form a cake that's 8 layers high. Cover the entirety with the last of the cream, then pat on the crumbs to coat. It'll be messy—there's no way of avoiding it.

Chill for at least 6 hours or, preferably, overnight. I think this cake is best eaten after it's had time to settle—the flavors melded, and softened. Leftovers will keep, covered, in the refrigerator for 3 to 5 days.

the sixth sense

Despite a good amount of sugar, this isn't a very sweet cake. Sometimes I like to enrich those warm, dulcet tones by drizzling a dark, leathery honey onto the pillows of cream that hold each layer. Brushing with mead instead of whisky further amplifies.

Roasted Almond Caramel Slice

It's difficult to describe a caramel slice as anything but sweet, but it is capable of achieving depth. Roasted almonds are a great match for the condensed milk filling, generating warmth as well as a savory, nutty, and round undertone. Small squares are often more desirable than large—it is rich, and rightfully so.

/ *Makes 16 to 20 squares* /

FOR THE CRUST

⅓ cup (45 g) almonds

1 cup (125 g) all-purpose flour

¼ cup (55 g) light brown sugar

¼ teaspoon salt

½ cup (1 stick/115 g) unsalted butter, melted

FOR THE FILLING

2 (14-ounce/396 g) cans sweetened condensed milk

⅓ cup (115 g) golden or dark corn syrup

½ cup + 1 teaspoon (120 g) unsalted butter, cubed

2 teaspoons vanilla extract

1 teaspoon flaky sea salt

FOR THE GANACHE

1 cup (170 g) finely chopped dark chocolate

1 cup (240 ml) heavy cream

Flaky sea salt, for finishing

ADJUST a rack to the middle of the oven, then preheat it to 350°F (180°C). Grease and line an 8-inch (20-cm) square baking pan with parchment paper, leaving a slight overhang on the sides.

First, make the crust. Place the almonds onto a lined baking sheet. Roast for 10 to 12 minutes, until golden. Cool completely, then grind in a food processor to a meal. Tip into a large mixing bowl, along with the flour, light brown sugar, and salt. Pour in the butter and stir until the mixture is evenly moistened. Transfer into the prepared pan, compacting it into a flat layer with your fingertips. Bake for 15 to 17 minutes, until golden brown. Transfer to a wire rack and set aside to cool. Lower the temperature to 320°F (160°C).

Next, make the filling. Put the condensed milk, golden or dark corn syrup, butter, vanilla, and salt into a medium heavy-bottomed saucepan that's set over medium heat. Cook, stirring often, until melted. Raise the heat slightly. Continue to cook, stirring constantly as it likes to catch, until viscous, thick, and trailing, 3 to 4 more minutes. Pour over the crust, then return to the oven. Bake for 13 to 15 minutes, until lightly bubbling and caramelized. Remove and leave to cool on a wire rack, then loosely cover and chill thoroughly.

For the ganache, put the chocolate into a medium heatproof bowl. In a small saucepan, bring the cream to a simmer over medium heat. Stream it all over the chocolate, then stir, slowly, until smooth. Spread over the caramel top to coat. Return to the refrigerator and chill again until set, about an hour.

Use the overhanging parchment to lift the slab out and onto a cutting board. Flourish with flaky salt, then, with a warm, sharp knife, slice into 16 to 20 squares. Serve cold, or close to it. These will keep, stored in an airtight container, in the refrigerator for 3 to 5 days.

the sixth sense

To embitter the slice, slick the top with dark chocolate instead of ganache. It'll set into a hard shell and fracture when cut.

Walnut and Honey Semifreddo

FOR THE PRALINE

¾ cup + 2 tablespoons (125 g) walnuts

½ cup + 2 tablespoons (130 g) granulated sugar

FOR THE SEMIFREDDO

2 cups (480 ml) heavy cream

¼ cup (85 g) honey

2 tablespoons Nocino liqueur

1 teaspoon vanilla extract

½ cup (100 g) granulated sugar

6 large egg yolks

For me, few things are as sweet and sentimental as semifreddo. It's simple but elegant, and it has a power that lasts long after a mouthful has ended. I like mine with praline and honey, in addition to Nocino, an aromatic liqueur that's made from unripe walnuts. The amount used is only a nip, as it's intended for altering—apt, given the wild tales of its origin, of pious men who drink, then go on to speak with goddesses, goblins, and ghouls. Seek out a bottle and you'll understand why.

/ *Serves 6 to 8* /

Adjust a rack to the middle of the oven, then preheat it to 350°F (180°C).

To make the praline, scatter the walnuts into an even layer over a lined baking sheet. Roast for 8 to 10 minutes, until golden brown and fragrant. Cool completely.

Next, combine the sugar with ⅓ cup (80 ml) water in a medium saucepan that's set over medium-high heat. Bring to a boil and cook, without stirring, until an amber-hued liquid has formed. Remove and pour over the roasted walnuts. Set aside to harden, then chop rough or fine, depending on your toothsome preference.

To make the semifreddo, line an 8 x 4 x 3-inch (21 x 11 x 7-cm) loaf pan with a few layers of plastic wrap, leaving an overhang over the sides.

In the bowl of a stand mixer that's fitted with the whisk attachment, whip the cream, honey, liqueur, and vanilla to stable peaks on medium speed. Be careful not to overdo it. You want it supple enough to fold in later without too much resistance. Transfer to the refrigerator and chill until needed.

Next, put the sugar and ⅓ cup (80 ml) water into a medium saucepan. Attach a candy thermometer to the side. Heat over medium heat, swirling occasionally, until the granules have dissolved. Raise the heat to high and bring to a rapid boil. Continue to cook until the syrup has reached thread stage, around 230°F (110°C). Meanwhile, start whisking the egg yolks in the bowl of a stand mixer. Start on low at first, then increase the speed as the syrup nears temperature. Carefully stream the boiling syrup into the yolks, between the whisk and the side of the bowl. Turn the speed to high and continue to whisk until pale, thick, and tripled in volume. All the steam will have escaped, and the bowl will no longer be hot to the touch.

With a large rubber spatula, gently fold thirds of the whipped cream into the yolk mixture, trying to retain as much lightness and air as possible.

the sixth sense

Sometimes I prefer the taste of frozen cream, without too much interruption. Use half of the praline, reserving the rest for another use, or set aside for serving. For a greater edge, take the walnuts down to a darker roast. The slightest change transforms their tannic structure and offsets the sweetness of this semifreddo.

Fold in the praline. Scrape into the prepared pan, smoothing out the top with an offset palette knife. Cover with aluminum foil and freeze until firm, at least 8 hours or, preferably, overnight.

Unmold the semifreddo onto a serving plate. Slice with a warm, sharp knife and serve soon after. This will keep, covered, in the coldest part of the freezer for 5 days.

Caramel Pound Cake

FOR THE CARAMEL

⅓ cup (70 g) granulated sugar

½ cup (120 ml) heavy cream

2 tablespoons honey

FOR THE CAKE

1¼ cups + 1 teaspoon (160 g) all-purpose flour

1¼ cups (120 g) ground almonds

¾ teaspoon baking powder

¼ teaspoon salt

¾ cup (170 g) unsalted butter, softened at room temperature

¾ cup + 2½ tablespoons (200 g) light brown sugar

3 large eggs

1 teaspoon vanilla extract

Zest from ½ a small orange

FOR THE GLAZE

¼ cup (60 g) unsalted butter, cubed

1¼ cups (150 g) confectioners' sugar, sifted

1 tablespoon Cognac, optional

I use sugar to transform this simple cake. To bake is to rely on it, but for many reasons its taste is often overlooked as usefulness. It can shine as itself, and it should. The caramel that hydrates the batter concentrates the sweetness, but the final crumb is where the real intensity lies. Sacrifice the ends to reveal the gold inside.

/ *Serves 8* /

First, make the caramel. Put the sugar into a medium saucepan that's set over medium-high heat. Let it singe, agitating occasionally to ensure even coloring, until it has turned amber. Remove from the heat, and stream in the cream, whisking carefully to incorporate. It'll seize at first, then dissolve as it continues to heat. Stir in the honey. Return to the heat. Bring to a simmer, then remove and leave until completely cool, stirring occasionally.

Adjust a rack to the middle of the oven, then preheat it to 400°F (200°C). Grease and line a 9 x 5½-inch (23 x 13-cm) loaf pan with parchment paper, letting the paper slightly overhang the sides.

Sift the flour, ground almonds, baking powder, and salt into a medium mixing bowl.

In the bowl of a stand mixer that's fitted with the paddle attachment, or with handheld electric beaters, beat the butter and light brown sugar on medium speed until light and fluffy, 3 to 5 minutes. Pause to scrape down the bowl, then beat in the eggs, one at a time, incorporating well after each addition. Beat in the vanilla and zest. Lower the speed and tip in the dry ingredients. Beat until just combined. Slowly stream in the cooled caramel, then raise the speed to medium-high. Continue to beat until uniformly luscious. Scrape the batter into the prepared pan, smoothing out the top with an offset palette knife.

Bake for 10 minutes, then carefully pry open the oven door. With a sharp knife, make a long incision a few inches down the middle of the cake. Close, then immediately lower the temperature to 325°F (160°C). Continue to bake for about another hour, rotating halfway through, until deeply golden. A skewer inserted into the middle should come out with a few moist crumbs attached. Tent the top with aluminum foil if at any stage you're concerned about it taking on too much color. Remove and leave to cool for 10 minutes, then invert the cake out and onto a wire rack, and cool completely.

For the glaze, put the butter into a saucepan. Cook over medium-high heat, swirling often, until nutty brown. Pour into a small heatproof bowl, then add the confectioners' sugar and Cognac, if using. Whisk to incorporate, loosening with warm water, until thick but pourable.

Glaze the cake, let it settle, and serve soon after. This is best eaten on the day of making, but will keep, stored in an airtight container, at room temperature for 2 to 3 days.

Roasted Pumpkin Mace Pie

FOR THE PUMPKIN PURÉE

A small whole butternut squash, 1½ to 2 pounds (700 to 900 g)

Light brown sugar

Extra-virgin olive oil

FOR THE CRUST

½ cup (60 ml) ice water

1 teaspoon apple cider vinegar

1¼ cups (160 g) all-purpose flour

½ teaspoon fresh thyme leaves

¼ teaspoon salt

½ cup + 1 teaspoon (120 g) unsalted butter, cold and cut into ½-inch cubes

1 egg white, lightly whisked with 1 teaspoon water, for the wash

FOR THE FILLING

½ cup (110 g) light brown sugar

¼ cup (50 g) granulated sugar

3 large eggs

1 teaspoon ground mace

1 teaspoon vanilla extract

1 tablespoon whisky, optional

¾ cup (180 ml) heavy cream

⅓ cup + 2 tablespoons (110 g) crème fraîche, plus more for serving

I don't fault a pumpkin pie—even the timid are brilliant. There are some desserts that provoke regardless—this is one—and it's anything but shy.

Butternut squash loves to be affected by heat. I roast them skin and all, which allows the flesh to tenderize under the weighted shell and caramelize, deeply. Those sinister shades stain this pie and make it unforgettable, in part thanks to mace, the feverish little sister of nutmeg. With a name so fraught with apprehension, she has a reputation that precedes her. Yet the spice is delicate, refined, and layered, with a soft warmth important for tempering sweetness.

/ *Serves 8* /

Adjust a rack to the middle of the oven, then preheat it to 400°F (200°C). Line a baking sheet with parchment paper.

Split the squash down the middle. Scatter the halves with light brown sugar, tailoring your pinch to their size. Drizzle with oil and place them onto the sheet, cut side facing down. Roast for about an hour, until tender and caramelized. Cool, then discard the seeds and scoop out the flesh. Transfer to a food processor or blender and purée until smooth. Re-measure it. You'll need 1¾ cups (430 g) for this recipe. Leftovers can be sealed and stored in the refrigerator for up to 5 days, or frozen for a few months.

Next, make the crust. Stir together the ice water and vinegar in a small bowl. Place in the refrigerator and chill until needed. Put the flour, thyme, and salt into a large mixing bowl. Add the butter and toss to coat. With a pastry blender or metal spatula, cut the cubes into the dry ingredients until it resembles mostly pebble-sized pieces. Drizzle in a few tablespoons of the ice water mixture. Stir to incorporate, then continue to add it in, a little at a time, until the mixture holds when pinched and squeezed. Some dry and flaky bits should remain. Shape into a ball, incorporating a few more drops of water if needed. Pat into a disc, then cover with plastic wrap. Chill in the refrigerator for at least an hour.

Set a 9-inch (23-cm) pie dish onto a rimmed baking sheet. Unwrap the dough onto a floured work surface and lightly dust the top. Roll it out into a circle that's about ⅛ inch (.3-cm) thick and a few inches larger than the dish that you're using. Carefully fit, then trim an inch off the overhang. Flute or crimp as desired. Freeze, while the oven preheats to 425°F (220°C).

Line the crust with a piece of parchment paper. Fill with ceramic weights or dried beans. Bake for 20 minutes, or until set. Remove and cool, then lift out the weights. Brush thinly with the egg wash and prick the base a few times with a fork. Return to the oven and bake for another 8 to 10 minutes, until golden brown. Remove and cool on a wire rack. Lower the temperature to 350°F (180°C).

For the filling, whisk together the pumpkin purée, light brown sugar, granulated sugar, eggs, mace, vanilla, and whisky, if using. Whisk in the cream and crème fraîche until silky smooth. Strain through a fine-mesh sieve into the cooled crust, filling it almost to the brim.

Bake for 45 to 55 minutes, until puffed and the edges are set. The middle should still retain a slight wobble. Leave to cool at room temperature for about 2 hours. Serve slices of the pie with crème fraîche on the side. This is best eaten on the day of making. Keep leftovers loosely covered in the refrigerator for 2 to 3 days.

the sixth sense

Traditional pies often use sweet, docile, and sometimes stale spices, and though the tiniest pinch is only ever needed, it does form the spine. Make it a strong one. There are some spices that resonate deeply for me—mace is one, ras el hanout another, and piment d'Espelette. Blended or sole, seek out what heat speaks to you.

Sticky Date and Stout Pudding

FOR THE CAKE

1¼ cups (200 g) soft dried pitted dates, chopped

1 teaspoon baking soda

1¼ cups + 1 teaspoon (160 g) all-purpose flour

2 teaspoons baking powder

1 teaspoon ground cinnamon

½ teaspoon ground ginger

¼ teaspoon ground allspice

¼ teaspoon salt

½ cup (1 stick/115 g) unsalted butter, softened at room temperature

¼ cup (55 g) dark brown sugar

2 tablespoons molasses

2 large eggs

FOR THE SAUCE

½ cup (1 stick/115 g) unsalted butter, cubed

1 cup (220 g) dark brown sugar

1 tablespoon molasses

¼ cup (60 ml) stout

½ cup (120 ml) heavy cream

I return to this recipe religiously each winter. Not just for the warmth, comfort, and taste, but for the eye-sense—it's alluring. The lumps and bumps that cleavage the top leave little to the imagination, but all below is not what it seems. Allow time for the pudding to rest, so that the sauce can swell the crumb. I find that the perfect point is somewhere between half an hour to an hour.

/ *Serves 6 to 8* /

Adjust a rack to the middle of the oven, then preheat it to 350°F (180°C). Grease a deep 9-inch (23-cm) ceramic baking dish with butter.

To make the cake, put the dates, baking soda, and ¾ cup (180 ml) boiling water into a medium heatproof bowl. Give it a stir, then cover and leave to soften and plump for about 10 minutes. Mash with a fork to a murky pulp, then set aside until cooled.

Sift the flour, baking powder, cinnamon, ginger, allspice, and salt into a medium mixing bowl.

In the bowl of a stand mixer that's fitted with the paddle attachment, or using handheld electric beaters, beat the butter, dark brown sugar, and molasses on medium speed until light caramel in hue—the goal isn't to incorporate a lot of air, just to get it nice and creamy. Pause to scrape down the bowl, then beat in the eggs, one at a time, incorporating well after each addition. Lower the speed, then tip in the dry ingredients and beat to a thick batter. Beat in the date mixture until uniform. Scrape into the prepared dish, smoothing it out to the edges with an offset palette knife. Bake for 30 to 35 minutes, until springy to the touch.

While the cake bakes, make the sauce. In a medium saucepan set over gentle heat, melt together the butter, dark brown sugar, molasses, and stout, whisking constantly to encourage even disintegration. Whisk in the cream. Continue to cook until the sauce is hot, viscous, and bubbling. Turn off the heat, and set aside.

As soon as the cake has left the oven, pierce several holes over it with a wooden skewer or tip of a sharp knife. Drench in sauce. Leave to swell and absorb for 30 minutes, or up to an hour. Serve slightly warm, with ice cream.

Pain d'Épices

Pain d'épices presents as more bread than cake. It's dark, brooding, and despite all the sugar, barely sweet, made with an assortment of spices that distinguish the mark of the chef. Mine is somewhat faithful to tradition and strikes at the heart of what it means to be gingerbread. The irregular pulse within comes from buckwheat flour, which creates a resilient yet tender crumb. As such, this will keep for a while, during which time the taste will intensify.

/ *Serves 8* /

FOR THE CAKE

1¼ cups + 1 teaspoon (160 g) all-purpose flour

¾ cup (90 g) buckwheat flour

1¼ teaspoons baking powder

¾ teaspoon baking soda

2 teaspoons ground cinnamon

½ teaspoon ground allspice

½ teaspoon ground ginger

¼ teaspoon ground cloves

¼ teaspoon ground nutmeg

A pinch of finely ground black pepper

¼ teaspoon salt

¼ cup (60 g) unsalted butter, cubed

1 cup (340 g) honey

½ cup (110 g) light brown sugar

1 large egg

FOR THE GLAZE

¼ cup (80 g) fig jam or orange marmalade

Juice from ½ an orange

1 tablespoon Cognac, optional

Adjust a rack to the middle of the oven, then preheat it to 350°F (180°C). Grease and line a 9 x 5½-inch (23 x 13-cm) loaf pan with parchment paper, leaving a slight overhang on the sides.

To make the cake, sift together the flour, buckwheat, baking powder, baking soda, cinnamon, allspice, ginger, cloves, nutmeg, pepper, and salt in a medium mixing bowl.

Put the butter, honey, and light brown sugar into a large saucepan, along with ⅔ cup (160 ml) water. Set it over medium heat and stir with a wooden spoon until dissolved. Stream the liquids into the dry ingredients, whisking in a clockwise motion, until uniform. Whisk in the egg. Pour the batter into the prepared pan.

Bake for 50 minutes to an hour, rotating halfway through, until deeply golden. A skewer inserted into the middle should come out clean. Cool for 10 minutes, then lift the cake out and onto a wire rack to cool completely.

To make the glaze, heat the jam or marmalade, orange juice, and Cognac, if using, in a small saucepan until homogenous. Slick the cake while it's warm, before slicing and serving. It'll keep loosely covered, at room temperature, for 5 days to a week.

Crème Brûlée Ice Cream

FOR THE ICE CREAM

2 cups (480 ml) whole milk

1⅔ cups (400 ml) heavy cream

1 vanilla bean

7 large egg yolks

⅔ cup (135 g) granulated sugar

A pinch of salt

FOR THE CAGE

½ cup (100 g) granulated sugar

1 tablespoon glucose syrup

I adore crème brûlée for the creaminess, as well as the grandiose use of vanilla. I also adore the cracked shell. Like casting a spell, here, the sugar is burnt, then flicked and spun in the air to create a nest of caramelized strands capable of enclosing the ice cream beneath. The base is a little different, made like a baked custard as inspired by Pierre Hermé. It creates a texture that's effortlessly light, with all the best reminders of a crème brûlée, but in a breathtaking new form.

/ *Serves 4* /

To make the ice cream, pour the milk and cream into a large saucepan. Split open the vanilla bean and scrape in the seeds, then toss in the pod too. Bring to a simmer over medium heat, then remove and set aside to infuse for an hour.

Adjust a rack to the middle of the oven, then preheat it to 250°F (120°C). Set out two large roasting dishes. The custard should fill them both about an inch (2.5 cm) of the way high, so choose vessels that are deep and wide.

In a large heatproof bowl, whisk together the egg yolks, sugar, and salt until pale and thick. Place a fine-mesh sieve over the top, then strain through the infused liquid. Whisk slowly to incorporate, then evenly divide between the roasting dishes. Bake for 40 to 45 minutes, until just set but still with a tremor. Cool, then cover and chill thoroughly, at least 8 hours, but preferably overnight.

Place a container or aluminum loaf pan into the freezer to keep cold. Scrape the custards into a blender and whir on the lowest speed until silky smooth and fluid once more. Transfer to an ice cream machine and churn according to the manufacturer's instructions. Extract into your par-frozen container, then cover with aluminum foil and freeze for a few hours, until firm.

For the cage, set two wooden spoons onto the kitchen counter, separating them a few hand spaces apart. Position the handles out over the edge, then stick the bases down to the counter with tape. Line the floor beneath with a few sheets of parchment paper. Fill a large heatproof bowl with cold water and ice.

Put the sugar and glucose syrup into a medium saucepan, along with ¼ cup (60 ml) water. Heat over medium-high heat, stirring often, until dissolved. Raise the heat and continue to cook, swirling occasionally but

without stirring, until the liquid is amber. Immediately plunge the pan into the bowl of ice water to hinder it from tainting further, then remove and stand for a minute or so until it can drip and thread like honey. Take a fork, dip it into the sugar, and flick it back and forth over the handles, quick and continuously.

Gather the strands into a nest-like amalgam. Serve with the ice cream, enclosing it. This is best eaten on the day of making, but can be kept, covered, in the coldest part of the freezer for about 5 days. The sugar must be spun prior to serving.

Toska Cake

FOR THE TOPPING

½ cup (1 stick/115 g) unsalted butter, cubed

1 cup (220 g) light brown sugar

⅓ cup (80 ml) heavy cream

Zest from ½ an orange

2 cups (230 g) flaked almonds

FOR THE CAKE

1 teaspoon green cardamom pods

1¼ cups (155 g) all-purpose flour

¾ teaspoon baking powder

¼ teaspoon salt

1 cup (260 g) almond paste

¾ cup + 2 tablespoons (180 g) granulated sugar

¾ cup (170 g) unsalted butter, softened at room temperature

4 large eggs, lightly whisked together

1 teaspoon flaky sea salt

This cake may be *toscakaka*, or Swedish almond paste cake, but I've derived the root from someplace else. *Toska*, in my mother tongue, or as Nabokov would tell it, is the embodiment of bittersweet. A word to describe a state of being so fueled with melancholia, love, and loss, the experience is necessary, if not vital, for flourishing. The caramelized-almond top protects a crumb so soft that it almost seems like a fault. But that's not without intention. Sweet, but biting, each mouthful is a delight.

/ *Serves 8* /

Adjust a rack to the middle of the oven, then preheat it to 350°F (180°C). Grease and line an 8-inch (20-cm) cake pan with parchment paper.

To make the topping, put the butter, light brown sugar, cream, and zest into a medium saucepan that's set over medium heat. Heat, stirring often, until dissolved. Stir in the almonds and let the mixture come to a loose bubble and boil, still stirring. Immediately remove, then pour it into the base of the prepared pan. Set aside while you make the batter.

Put the cardamom into a skillet that's set over medium heat. Toast, shaking often, until the pods have split and taken on a faded hue. Cool, then extract the seeds. Grind in a mortar and pestle to a fine powder. Transfer to a medium bowl, then sift over the flour, baking powder, and salt.

Break up the almond paste. Add it to the bowl of a stand mixer that's fitted with the paddle attachment, along with the sugar. Beat on medium-high speed until clumpy, then add the butter. Beat to a light and fluffy paste, 3 to 5 minutes. Pause to scrape down the bowl, then lower the speed and slowly stream in the eggs. Beat until homogenous, then tip in the dry ingredients and beat until well combined. Scrape the batter into the prepared pan, smoothing it out with an offset spatula over the almond layer.

Bake for 1 to 1¼ hours. Because of the top, it'll be hard to tell when it's done. A skewer inserted into the middle should come out clean from crumbs and sticky with caramel. Let cool in the pan for 15 minutes, then carefully invert onto a serving plate.

Serve just warm or at room temperature, sprinkled with flaky salt. This is best eaten on the day of making but will keep, stored in an airtight container, at room temperature for 2 days.

Sour

To eat sour is to understand fraught. I find that it is the most misunderstood of the five tastes, striking and defiant, but we begin on it from birth and so it shall continue on. ¶ Our first thought is hunger, our first sip is milk, our first sense is sweet, and then sour. It's the instinctual taste of succulence, elicited from such puckerish places like citrus, in lemons and limes, or more covert in forbidden fruit, as plums, cherries, and berries will attest. Sour forms the basis of all fermentation, which would not be itself without the wild tang, and that I rely on to provide a line of clarity in dessert. I think of spilled milk, one of the most beautiful phrases in the English language, and then of her, who I loved, deeply. ¶ The rotting of the organic creates sourness, as if loss were a parasite stealing sustenance from the plum, or the aphid draining out sweet sap. Drip, drop, the tightly wound taste bursts, and leaks, and though it seems contradictory, sour adores sugar. I could warn small doses, but rarely do I use it like that; thick strips of citrus peel, a twist of the whole fruit, heavenly lactic contortions—I know I have done well when I still feel it on the tips of my teeth. ¶ Bite into a sour thing under the assumption that it's sweet and you'll know surprise, with a rush of sensations that soon follow. *Tart, light, unpredictable. Bright, tingling, effervescent. The essence of destruction but also creation.* There are many synonyms for it, and these alter our perception. To me, sourness speaks as if it asks to be soothed, and plays out in the mouth like a scene from the wrong script, which is not without satisfaction for it was written by my hand. It is a taste vital to telling the full tale of my desserts; fragile if not handled with care—healed if it is.

Mikada

FOR THE CAKE

5 cups (625 g) all-purpose flour

1 cup + 1 teaspoon (125) buckwheat flour

A pinch of salt

1 cup (2 sticks/230 g) unsalted butter, softened at room temperature

1¼ cups (250 g) granulated sugar

3 large eggs

Zest from 1 lemon

1¼ cups (300 g) sour cream

FOR ASSEMBLY

¼ cup (45 g) finely grated white chocolate

1 cup + 3 tablespoons (200 g) melted white chocolate

FOR THE CREAM

5 cups (1200 ml) heavy cream

1¼ cups (300 g) sour cream

¾ cup (150 g) granulated sugar

1 teaspoon vanilla extract

The bones of this recipe belong to the old world, to a generation of women who sated hunger from almost nothing. Sourness formed their survival and was put forth to me as poetic, even as a child. In Russian, that translates well into food—sweet or not, no meal is ever complete without sour cream. It exists as more than just fermented dairy, it's a lifeline. In this cake, it thrums, adding lightness and richness without the risk of overwhelm. I don't doubt that I will never be able to fully understand the reality of my heritage, but no mind, for I inherited its tongue.

/ *Serves 12 to 16* /

First, make the cake layers. In a large mixing bowl, combine the flours and salt.

In the bowl of a stand mixer that's fitted with the paddle attachment, or using handheld electric beaters, cream the butter and sugar on medium speed until light and fluffy, 3 to 5 minutes. Scrape down the bowl, then beat in the eggs, one at a time, incorporating well after each addition. Beat in the zest and sour cream. The mixture should seem thin and curdled but will come together as you continue to work. Lower the speed, then tip in the dry ingredients and beat until incorporated. Knead to unify the dough, then cover and rest in the refrigerator for about an hour.

Line three 9½ x 13-inch (24 x 33-cm) rimmed quarter-sheet pans with parchment paper. Adjust racks to the top, middle, and bottom thirds of the oven, then preheat it to 350°F (180°C).

Turn the dough out onto a floured work surface. Divide it into seven equal portions, keeping three on the table, re-covering the rest and returning them to the refrigerator to keep cold. Roll each to about the size of the prepared pans, flouring as needed to prevent sticking. Transfer and trim to fit and patch any tears with scraps. It doesn't have to be perfect, as the cake will be filled, covered, and trimmed upon finishing, but as close as possible.

Bake for 14 to 16 minutes, until golden brown. Cool for 10 minutes, before lifting off and onto a wire rack, while you repeat the above process with the remaining dough. You should have 7 layers in total.

Take the roughest looking layer, and, with your fingertips, break it down to a fine crumb in a large mixing bowl. Stir in the grated white chocolate. Set aside for assembly.

(cont.)

Brush the melted white chocolate over the tops of the remaining layers, and leave to set.

To make the cream, in the bowl of a stand mixer that's fitted with the whisk attachment, whip the cream, sour cream, sugar, and vanilla to soft but stable peaks on medium speed.

When you're ready to assemble, set a first cake layer onto a serving board, chocolate side facing up. Spoon over a few tablespoons of the whipped cream, spreading it all the way to the edges with an offset palette knife, then press on a second layer, chocolate side facing down. Again, spread thinly with cream, and re-layer. Repeat this process until all of the layers have been used. Coat the top of the cake in the last of the cream—you should have a little left over after filling—then take the crumble mixture and press it on to stick. Chill for at least 8 hours, but preferably overnight.

When you're ready to serve, trim off the edges of the cake with a sharp serrated knife to reveal the hidden layers. Cut into squares—the portion a reflection of desire. This will keep, loosely covered, in the refrigerator for 3 days.

Buckwheat Brioche

FOR THE DOUGH

4 cups (500 g) all-purpose flour

½ cup + 1 tablespoon (65 g) buckwheat flour

⅓ cup + 1½ tablespoons (85 g) granulated sugar

4½ teaspoons (14 g) instant dried yeast

1 teaspoon salt

3 large eggs

⅓ cup + 1½ tablespoons (100 ml) whole milk

¾ cup + 1 teaspoon (175 g) unsalted butter, softened at room temperature

FOR THE WASH

1 large egg

1 large egg yolk

2 tablespoons whole milk

A pinch of salt

Granulated sugar, for sprinkling

The best bit about this bread is the shattering crust, which encloses an impossibly soft interior. The use of buckwheat is important not just for taste, but also to retain integrity and structure, and it imparts a soured tang so redolent of my childhood. The crumb will firm the longer it stands—best eaten warm, but also good for toasting or, better, pain perdu.

/ ***Serves 6 to 8*** /

First, make the dough. Put the flours, sugar, yeast, and salt into the bowl of a stand mixer that's fitted with the dough hook attachment. Mix on low speed to combine, then add the eggs and milk. Knead on medium speed for a few more minutes, until a rough and shaggy dough has pulled together. Add the butter, a tablespoon at a time, waiting until blended before adding the next. Raise the speed and continue to knead until a smooth and elastic ball has formed. With a few pulls and stretches, bring it together into a ball. Transfer to a greased large bowl, then cover and leave to rise in a warm spot until doubled in size, 1½ to 2 hours.

Grease and line a 9 x 5 x 3-inch (23 x 13 x 7-cm) loaf pan with parchment paper.

Split the dough. Shape each half into a taut ball, pulling and tucking to create a seam at the base with your hand. Position into the prepared pan, spacing well apart. Re-cover, and leave to rise again, but this time until just under doubled—anywhere from 30 minutes to an hour.

Adjust a rack to the middle of the oven, then preheat it to 350°F (180°C).

Whisk together the egg, yolk, milk, and salt for the wash. Brush the top of the risen loaf, then sprinkle with sugar. Bake for 35 to 40 minutes, until golden brown. A skewer inserted into the middle should come out clean. Cool in the pan for 15 minutes, then turn out and onto a wire rack to cool further, before serving warm or at room temperature. This should be eaten on the day of making, but leftovers can be stored, tightly covered, in the refrigerator for about 3 days. Warm slightly, for its best.

Buttermilk Pancakes with Wine Butter

FOR THE WINE BUTTER

1⅔ cups (400 ml) light-bodied red wine

1 cup (2 sticks/230 g) unsalted cultured butter, softened at room temperature

A pinch of flaky sea salt

FOR THE PANCAKES

2¼ cups (280 g) all-purpose flour

1 teaspoon baking powder

1 teaspoon baking soda

½ teaspoon salt

¼ cup (50 g) granulated sugar

2 cups (480 ml) buttermilk

2 large eggs, separated

1 teaspoon vanilla extract

3 tablespoons unsalted butter, melted

Vegetable oil, for cooking the pancakes

Few things, I think, are capable of generating as much residual heat in the mind as pancakes on a Sunday morning. They're sacred, personal, and not to be messed with. The technique of whisking the whites to soft peaks seems like an additional step, but it's crucial to achieve that elusive cloud-like mouthfeel. The pancakes are brought back down to earth by a wine butter, which I could make for the blush alone.

/ *Makes about 12 pancakes* /

For the wine butter, pour the wine into a deep saucepan. Bring to a simmer over medium heat, then lower the heat slightly. Continue to cook, swirling from time to time, until reduced to a viscous liquid, about half an hour. It shouldn't be so resistant that it catches the bottom of the pan, but just bodied enough to cling to the back of a spoon. Pour into a medium heatproof bowl, and leave to cool completely. Re-measure it. You'll need ¼ cup (60 ml) for this recipe.

In the bowl of a stand mixer that's fitted with the paddle attachment, beat the butter for a few minutes on medium-high speed until pale, slick, and silky—like mayonnaise. Pause to scrape down the bowl, then beat in the reduced wine until homogenous. Add the flaky salt. Continue to beat until aerated.

Scrape the whipped butter into a small bowl, cover with plastic wrap, and leave at room temperature until needed. Use this soon after making for best results, as it will firm with time, but it can also be made in advance and refrigerated, though it will lose softness.

To make the pancakes, sift the flour, baking powder, soda, and salt into a large bowl, then stir in the sugar. Use a wooden spoon to push and shove the dry ingredients aside to form a well in the middle. In a separate large bowl or pouring jug, whisk together the buttermilk, egg yolks, vanilla, and butter until smooth. Set both mixtures aside.

Next, in the bowl of a stand mixer that's fitted with the whisk attachment, or with a handheld electric whisk, whisk the egg whites to soft and foamy peaks. Stream the milky-yolk mixture into the well of the dry ingredients, whisking slowly and with a strong guiding hand, until just incorporated. Some small lumps are fine to remain, if not ideal. With a large rubber spatula and as little agitation as possible, fold in the egg whites until streak-free.

Position a cast-iron skillet over medium heat and pour in enough vegetable oil to lightly coat it. Using a ⅓ cup (80 ml) measuring cup, portion the batter into the pan, leaving a few inches of space apart. Cook the pancakes, a few at a time, until small bubbles have risen to the surface, 2 to 3 minutes, then flip and cook for a minute or so longer, until golden. Stack onto a plate while you finish with the remaining batter.

Serve warm, soon after, with wine butter.

Plum Parfait

FOR THE PLUMS

About 6 (350 g) small dark plums, halved and pitted

¼ cup (50 g) granulated sugar

Juice from ½ a lemon

¼ cup (60 ml) umeshu (see below)

FOR THE PARFAIT

1¼ cups (300 ml) heavy cream

¼ cup (60 g) plain Greek yogurt

1 teaspoon vanilla extract

½ teaspoon cracked black pepper

¾ cup + 2 teaspoons (160 g) granulated sugar

4 large egg yolks

the sixth sense

Umeshu is a Japanese liqueur made from unripe ume, which, to me, seem like an apricot-plum hybrid. It's sweet and sour, and often comes bottled with the bloated fruit inside. They're not purely ornamental—you can fish them out, slice them fine, and eat them with this.

Parfait means perfect, and this one is especially so. It's plummy, peppered, and cooling, ideal for dog days, when the sultry dregs of summer stagger on. The only real cooking to be done is a little roasting for the fruit—blasted hot, it will be over fast. Time takes care of the rest. Start this recipe early, so it's ready for the golden hour of an afternoon.

/ ***Serves 8*** /

PREHEAT the oven to 400°F (200°C).

In a large mixing bowl, toss together the plums, sugar, lemon juice, and umeshu. Transfer to a deep roasting dish, shuffling the fruit into an even layer. Tent with aluminum foil. Roast for 25 to 35 minutes, agitating halfway through, until tender. Remove and cool completely.

Line a 9 x 5½-inch (23 x 13-cm) loaf pan with a few layers of plastic wrap, leaving a sling over the sides.

For the parfait, in the bowl of a stand mixer that's fitted with the whisk attachment, whip the cream, yogurt, vanilla, and black pepper to soft peaks on medium speed. Keep cold in the refrigerator until needed.

Put the sugar and ⅔ cup (160 ml) water into a deep saucepan. Bring to a boil over medium heat, stirring often to dissolve the granules. Raise the heat to high and cook until the syrup reaches 230°F (110°C) on a candy thermometer. You can test for doneness by dropping a teaspoon into a glass of cold water—when it drips down into elongated threads, it's ready. Meanwhile, start whisking the egg yolks in the bowl of a stand mixer that's set on medium speed. As soon as the syrup reaches temperature, add it into the yolks, pouring it between the whisk and the side of the bowl. Raise the speed to medium-high. Continue to whisk until pale, thick, and almost tripled in volume, about 5 minutes.

Using a large rubber spatula, fold a third of the whipped cream into the yolk mixture. Fold in another third, followed by the last, until just combined. Tenderly fold in the plums—you want some streaks to remain. Scrape into the prepared pan. Cover with aluminum foil and freeze until solid, at least 8 hours, but preferably overnight.

Pry the parfait out of the pan using the sling, then position it onto a plate and unwrap. Slice thickly with a warm knife. Allow a few minutes to stand and soften before serving. This will keep, covered, in the coldest part of the freezer for 5 days.

Black Currant Cheesecake

FOR THE BASE

2 cups (130 g) plain chocolate biscuits

1 tablespoon granulated sugar

1 teaspoon coffee powder

A pinch of salt

¼ cup (60 g) unsalted butter, melted

FOR THE FILLING

2¼ cups (500 g) cream cheese, softened at room temperature

⅔ cup (135 g) granulated sugar

3 large eggs

1 teaspoon vanilla extract

1 cup + 2 tablespoons (190 g) melted dark chocolate

¾ cup (180 g) sour cream

¼ cup (60 ml) heavy cream

2 tablespoons hot espresso

FOR THE BLACK CURRANTS

1½ cups (160 g) black currants

⅓ cup (70 g) granulated sugar

¼ cup (60 ml) crème de cassis liqueur

Juice of ½ a lemon

1 star anise

Not for the faint of heart—I really do think this cake could stop one. It's rich and intense, hard to isolate the striking source. Black currants, dark chocolate, and coffee are kindred spirits, and all share a similar tannic, as well as sharp, sour, and acidulated profile, which enhances the dairy. Like for like when pairing, I say.

/ *Serves 8* /

Adjust a rack to the middle of the oven, then preheat it to 350°F (180°C). Grease and line an 8-inch (20-cm) round springform cake pan with parchment paper, encasing the outside with a few layers of aluminum foil. Bring a kettle of water to a boil.

Make the base. Blitz the biscuits to a fine crumb in a food processor, then re-measure. You should have about 1 cup's worth. Tip into a medium mixing bowl, then add the sugar, coffee powder, and salt. Pour in the butter and stir until evenly moistened. Transfer into the prepared pan, pressing the mixture into a flat and even layer with the back of a spoon. Bake for 10 to 12 minutes, until a gradient darker around the edges. Cool on a wire rack while you make the filling.

Lower the temperature to 250°F (120°C). Pour enough boiling water into a deep roasting dish until it's about halfway full, then set it on the oven floor.

For the filling, in the bowl of a stand mixer that's fitted with the paddle attachment, or using handheld electric beaters, beat the cream cheese on medium speed for a minute or so until smooth and malleable. Pause to scrape down the bowl, then add the sugar. Beat until light and fluffy, then one at a time, beat in the eggs, followed by the vanilla. Again, pause to scrape, then lower the mixer speed. Stream in the chocolate. Beat until just combined, then beat in the sour cream, cream, and espresso. If at any point the chocolate seizes, it can be fixed. Set the bowl over a double boiler and gently heat until any hardened parts have melted. Return to the stand mixer, and beat again until luscious. Pass the filling through a fine-mesh sieve into the prepared pan, smoothing it out with an offset palette knife.

Bake for 1¼ hours, or until just set but still with a slight tremble in the middle. Turn off the oven and carefully remove the dish of water. Leave the cheesecake to rest inside with the door propped open until it has come to room temperature. Transfer to the refrigerator, and chill thoroughly.

For the black currants, tip the fruit into a medium saucepan, along with the sugar, liqueur, lemon juice, and star anise. Bring to a simmer over medium heat, stirring often until slumped. Cool completely.

To serve, release the cheesecake from the pan and slide it onto a plate. Tentatively peel off the paper. Adorn with stewed black currants, then slice and serve. It will keep, loosely covered, in the refrigerator for 2 to 3 days.

Passion Fruit Pavlova

FOR THE CURD

⅔ cup (135 g) granulated sugar

Zest and juice from 2 small lemons

½ cup (120 ml) fresh passion fruit pulp, seeds strained

4 large egg yolks

¾ cup (170 g) unsalted butter, cubed

A pinch of salt

FOR THE MERINGUE

5 large egg whites

1½ cups (300 g) granulated sugar

1½ tablespoons cornstarch

1½ teaspoons white vinegar

1 teaspoon vanilla extract

FOR THE CREAM

1½ cups (360 ml) heavy cream

2 tablespoons granulated sugar

Seeds scraped from 1 vanilla bean

Passion fruit, split, to finish

Confectioners' sugar, to flourish

Spend enough time with this curd and you'll know sourness. Just straining the nectar from the seeds alone causes me to salivate. It does require a lot of passion fruit, so there are brief interludes in the year that I'm able to make it—but that's also the beauty. If the season hasn't been great, you can play with lemon, lime, orange, or even mandarin, but the sour scale will shift, and then how you choose to finish this pavlova should too. It's a recipe that invites all sorts of experimentation.

/ *Serves 6* /

To make the curd, rub the sugar and zest together in a medium heatproof bowl until fragrant. Add the juice, passion fruit pulp, and egg yolks. Stir to incorporate, then toss in the butter. Set the bowl over a saucepan that's filled with a few inches of barely simmering water, making sure that the base of the bowl does not touch the water below. Whisk slowly and constantly over medium heat until glossy, viscous, and trailing, about 10 to 12 minutes. Whisk in the salt. Strain the curd through a fine-mesh sieve into a medium heatproof bowl, then cover the surface with plastic wrap. Refrigerate until set, 8 hours, but preferably overnight.

Adjust a rack to the middle of the oven, then preheat it to 300°F (150°C). Line a baking sheet with parchment paper.

To make the meringue, in the bowl of a stand mixer that's fitted with the whisk attachment, whisk the egg whites on medium speed until soft and foamy. Add the sugar a heaping tablespoon at a time, waiting until all incorporated before adding the next. Whisk to thick and glossy peaks. Fold in the cornstarch, vinegar, and vanilla. Scrape the meringue onto the prepared sheet, swirling it into a mound that's about 8 inches (20 cm) in diameter. Hollow out a slight cavity in the center. Transfer to the oven and immediately reduce the temperature to 250°F (120°C).

Bake for 1½ hours, or until crisp to the touch. Turn off the oven and pry open the door, leaving the meringue inside to cool completely in the residual heat.

When you're ready to assemble, in the bowl of a stand mixer that's fitted with the whisk attachment, whip the cream, sugar, and vanilla seeds to supple peaks on medium speed. Slide the meringue onto a plate. Spoon the whipped cream into the cavity, layering it with curd and the split passion fruit. Dust with confectioners' sugar, then serve. It'll keep, stored in an airtight container in the refrigerator, for 1 to 2 days.

Citron Tart

FOR THE CRUST

2 cups (250 g) all-purpose flour

⅔ cup (80 g) confectioners' sugar

½ teaspoon salt

¾ cup (170 g) unsalted butter, cold and cut into ½-inch (1.3-cm) cubes

3 large egg yolks

1 large egg, lightly whisked, for the wash

FOR THE FILLING

1⅓ cups + 1 tablespoon (280 g) granulated sugar

Zest from 2 lemons

½ cup (120 ml) lemon juice

¼ cup (60 ml) yuzu juice

1 cup (2 sticks/230 g) unsalted butter, cubed

6 large eggs

6 large egg yolks

A pinch of salt

The face of this tart is far from ideal, but that's what makes it perfect. The yuzu inside is the star; strong, sour, and citric—it bursts. It can also handle heat. The technique of scorching was inspired by chef Theo Randall's striking Amalfi lemon tart, the yuzu posturing as a surrogate for the prized Italian fruit. A pinch of salt will lessen the sting—or finish it with a flourish of singed lemon powder (page 112) for greater smoke.

/ *Serves 8* /

To make the crust, whisk together the flour, confectioners' sugar, and salt in a large mixing bowl. Add the butter and toss to coat. Rub and blend the cubes into the dry ingredients until they are in mostly pebble-sized pieces. Add the yolks and stir them in to combine, then gather the dough into a ball. Shape into a disc. Wrap, then chill for an hour or up to a day.

Position a 10-inch (25-cm) tart tin that's about 1¼ inches (3.5 cm) deep with a removable base onto a baking sheet. Unwrap the dough onto a floured work surface and dust the top. With a wooden pin, begin to roll it out into a circle that's about ⅛ inch (.3 cm) thick and a few inches larger than the tin that you're using. Transfer and fit, then trim off the excess overhang. Freeze, while the oven preheats to 350°F (180°C).

Line the crust with a sheet of parchment paper, then fill it to the brim with ceramic weights or dried beans. Bake for 20 minutes, or until dry and set. Cool slightly, then remove the paper and weights. Brush lightly with egg wash. Return to the oven and continue to bake for another 8 to 10 minutes, until golden. Cool on a wire rack while you make the filling.

Preheat the broiler to high. Put the sugar and zest into a medium heatproof bowl and rub the mixture together until fragrant. Stir in the lemon and yuzu juices, followed by the butter. Lightly whisk the eggs and yolks together, then add them into the bowl, along with the salt. Set over a saucepan that's filled with a few inches of barely simmering water. Do not let the base touch the water below. Stir constantly over medium-low heat, until thick enough to coat the back of a spoon. It should be glossy, golden, and softly set, like curd. Strain into the crust.

Place the tart under the broiler. Broil until black splotches appear, 3 to 5 minutes. Serve chilled or at room temperature, sliced thick or thin—depending on how sour you like it. It'll keep, loosely covered, in the refrigerator for 3 days.

Singed Sherbet Meringues

4 lemons

A pinch of salt

FOR THE MERINGUES

⅔ cup (135 g) granulated sugar

1 cup (120 g) confectioners' sugar, sifted

4 large egg whites, at room temperature

½ teaspoon cream of tartar

A pinch of salt

1 teaspoon rose water

FOR THE SHERBET

⅔ cup (80 g) confectioners' sugar, sifted

2 teaspoons citric acid

1 teaspoon singed lemon powder

¼ teaspoon baking soda

The risk of a thorn is well worth the rose, and so it is with these meringues. The sherbet that coats them is puckerish and fairy-dust-like, imparting an instant sour hit. But making it is a slow burn, as the lemon skins need time to wither under the heat. As such, it's potent, and a little bit goes far, but it's easier to make in great volume than small. Useful in sweet and savory contexts, you'll find yourself reaching for it more than you'd think.

/ *Makes 6 meringues* /

First, make the singed lemon powder. Preheat the oven to 170°F (80°C). Line a large baking sheet with parchment paper.

Wash, dry, and remove the peel in thin strips from your lemons, leaving as much white pith behind as possible. Place onto the prepared sheet in a single layer. Roast until dry and brittle—1½ to 2 hours, but really, the time it takes will depend on the thickness of the cut. I check in every half hour or so and adjust accordingly. They're done when the skin wants to snap rather than bend. Turn off the oven and leave to cool in the residual heat.

With a food processor or spice grinder, pulverize the peels to a fine powder, then add the salt. Seal in an airtight jar, and store in a cool, dark place for use over the next few months.

To make the meringues, start by adjusting racks to the top and bottom thirds of the oven, then preheat it to 250°F (120°C). Line two baking sheets with parchment paper.

Whisk both sugars together in a medium bowl until incorporated. Next, in the bowl of a stand mixer that's fitted with the whisk attachment, whisk the egg whites, cream of tartar, and salt on medium speed until soft and foamy peaks have formed. Add the sugar, scattering it in a tablespoon at a time. Whisk until thick and glossy, then whisk in the rose water.

Drop a few generous tablespoons of the meringue onto the prepared sheets, swirling it out and into ½-inch (1.25-cm) rough mounds with the back of the spoon. Leave a few inches of space apart for expansion. You should be able to fit 3 per sheet. Bake for 1¼ to 1½ hours, until dry to the touch. Turn off the oven and cool inside.

For the sherbet, stir all the ingredients together in a small bowl. Sift over the meringues, and dust with a further pinch of singed lemon powder. These will keep, stored in an airtight container, for 5 to 7 days.

Sparkling Cranberry Jelly

FOR THE CRÈME FRAÎCHE

2 cups (480 ml) heavy cream

⅔ cup (160 ml) buttermilk

FOR THE JELLY

2 cups + 2 tablespoons (510 ml) Crémant

1½ cups + 2 tablespoons (390 ml) cranberry juice

Juice from ½ a lemon

1 sprig of rosemary

1½ cups (300 g) granulated sugar

6 titanium-strength gelatin leaves

Indulgent, jewel-toned, and just stable, this isn't like the dull jellies that I remember from my childhood. Instead, it's a dessert of intricacies—more sour than sweet, silky instead of firm, and adulterated with wine. It goes to the head, so I like to serve it with some acidulated crème fraîche to cut through. It contrasts but doesn't distract. The setting time for both the jelly and cream is slow but worth it. You can time their creation up, then forget about dessert.

/ ***Serves 6 to 8*** /

START the crème fraîche, as it needs time to coagulate. In a large bowl, whisk together the cream and buttermilk just to incorporate. Cover with a few layers of cheesecloth and leave undisturbed at room temperature for 1 to 2 days, until tangy, silky, and thick. I find that the time it takes depends on your season and location—longer in the considerable winters of the cool-climate place where I live now, shorter in the humidity of where I used to exist. Stir to reawaken, then transfer to a jar or container. Seal, and refrigerate. It'll thicken as it chills, and keep for 5 days to a week.

For the jelly, put the Crémant, cranberry and lemon juices, and rosemary into a deep saucepan. Tip in the sugar. Set the pan over medium heat and bring to below a boil, stirring often to dissolve the granules. Reduce the heat and simmer slowly. Meanwhile, soften the gelatin in a small bowl of cold water for 5 minutes.

Slide the cranberry liquid off the heat. Squeeze the excess water from the gelatin and add it in, whisking well to dissolve. Pour into your desired vessel, keeping or discarding the sprig. Cover and refrigerate until set, about 8 hours, but preferably overnight.

Spoon the jelly into bowls and serve with crème fraîche. It'll keep, covered, in the refrigerator for 3 to 5 days.

the sixth sense

While I love ornate molded jellies, they demand a great deal of setting power, which I think sacrifices on flavor, aroma, and texture. Instead, this makes a soft-set kind, perfect for serving en masse in a glass vessel and seizing the herbaceous sprig or berries inside, if desired.

Coeur à la Crème

FOR THE HEART

1½ cups (340 g) cream cheese

½ cup (120 g) crème fraîche

⅔ cup (80 g) confectioners' sugar

Zest from 1 lemon

2 teaspoons vanilla extract

1 cup + 2 tablespoons (270 ml) heavy cream

FOR THE SAUCE

1 small sprig of rosemary

½ cup (100 g) granulated sugar

3 cups (375 g) raspberries

⅓ cup (80 ml) red wine

Juice and a thick strip of zest from 1 lemon

2 juniper berries

Fresh raspberries, for serving

Confectioners' sugar, for finishing

A rose petal, optional

the sixth sense

This is the perfect canvas for seasonal fruit. The creaminess takes an ardent liking to highly strung red fruits—red currants, cherries, or strawberries. But wherever your desire leads, be cautious with the wine. A light-bodied red, like pinot noir or gamay, goes well, and there'll be three-quarters of a bottle left after making this dessert, and though it does affront all laws of pairing, I drink the rest alongside it.

This heart isn't sweet, it's sour. Made from a mixture of rich dairies that are left to weep and then coagulate, this dessert is surrounded by a sea of sharp raspberry-red, and is so simple to make, yet it remains beguiling. A porcelain coeur à la crème mold is traditionally needed to form the shape, but it can also be organically crafted into position by hand, or fate. It needs to rest for it to be at its best, so plan ahead. At least eight hours for a soft heart, more time left hanging for a firm one.

/ *Serves 6* /

Set a coeur à la crème mold or a fine-mesh sieve into a rimmed dish. Line it with slightly dampened cheesecloth, allowing it to drape over the sides like a veil.

In the bowl of a stand mixer that's fitted with the paddle attachment, beat the cream cheese on medium speed for a minute or so, until smooth and malleable. Pause to scrape, then lower the speed. Beat in the crème fraîche, confectioners' sugar, zest, and vanilla until fluffy, 2 to 3 minutes. Again, scrape down the bowl, then switch out the paddle for the whisk attachment. Stream in the cream. Continue to whisk until the mixture is soft, silky, and supple, almost like underdone whipped cream. Scrape into the prepared mold, packing it in tightly. Sheath with more cheesecloth, then set a small plate over the top. Weigh it down with something heavy—condiment jars or so—to assist with the seep. Transfer to the refrigerator, and let the whey slowly drain out overnight.

For the sauce, blitz the rosemary with the granulated sugar in a spice grinder or food processor. Transfer to a medium saucepan, along with the raspberries, wine, lemon juice, and peel. Crush the juniper berries with the tip of a sharp knife and add them in too. Stir over medium-low heat until the raspberries have softened to the point of disintegration. The liquid should be reduced and syrup-like. Remove, and discard the aromatics, then purée with an immersion blender. Strain into a medium heatproof bowl, cover with plastic wrap, and chill until completely cold.

To serve, invert the heart into a shallow bowl, then remove the mold and cheesecloth. Pour in the red sauce to engulf. Stud with raspberries and dust with confectioners' sugar. Eat cold, adorned with a single rose petal. It will keep, loosely covered, in the refrigerator for up to 3 days.

Roasted Rhubarb Layer Cake

Rhubarb is a glorious thing. I like the tart robustness of the standard garden variety best, I think, when roasted down, which gives it the freedom to show off its weathered depth. This seems like a sweet cake, but the inside is bracing, and despite all the sugar, the sourness is not lost. It endures and becomes quite the sticking point.

/ *Serves 8 to 10* /

FOR THE CAKE

2 cups (250 g) cake flour

⅔ cup (65 g) ground almonds

2 teaspoons baking powder

½ teaspoon ground cardamom

¼ teaspoon salt

¾ cup + 1 teaspoon (175 g) unsalted butter, softened at room temperature

1½ cups (300 g) granulated sugar

5 large egg whites, lightly whisked

2 teaspoons vanilla extract

1 cup + 2 tablespoons (270 ml) whole milk

FOR THE SYRUP

½ cup (100 g) granulated sugar

Juice from 1 lemon

FOR THE RHUBARB

½ pound (240 g) rhubarb, cleaned, trimmed, and chopped into 2-inch (5-cm) pieces

¼ cup (50 g) granulated sugar

¼ cup (60 ml) gin

Juice from ½ a lemon

FOR THE BUTTERCREAM

5 large egg whites

1⅓ cups + 1 tablespoon (280 g) granulated sugar

1¾ cups (400 g) unsalted butter, softened at room temperature

¼ cup (60 g) crème fraîche

1 teaspoon rose water

ADJUST a rack to the middle of the oven, then preheat it to 350°F (180°C). Grease and line three 7-inch (18-cm) cake pans with parchment paper.

Make the cake. Sift the cake flour, almonds, baking powder, cardamom, and salt into a medium mixing bowl.

In the bowl of a stand mixer that's fitted with the whisk attachment, beat the butter and sugar on medium speed until light and fluffy, 3 to 5 minutes. Pause to scrape down the bowl, then resume mixing and slowly stream in the egg whites. Beat until well combined, then beat in the vanilla. Lower the speed. Tip in half of the dry ingredients and beat until just combined, then beat in all of the milk, followed by the last of the dry ingredients. Raise the speed and continue to beat for a further minute, until aerated. Divide the batter among the prepared pans, smoothing it out with an offset palette knife.

Bake for 30 to 35 minutes, until light golden brown. A skewer inserted into the middle of the cakes should come out clean. Leave to cool in the pans for 15 minutes, then turn out and onto a wire rack to cool completely.

Meanwhile, make the syrup. Put the sugar, lemon juice, and ¼ cup (60 ml) water into a small saucepan. Bring to a boil over medium heat, stirring often, until dissolved. Cool, then level off the domed cake tops with a serrated knife. Drench well with syrup.

To roast the rhubarb, preheat the oven to 400°F (200°C). Place the fruit into a ceramic baking dish. Scatter over the sugar and toss to coat. Pour over the gin and lemon juice. Tent the top with aluminum foil. Roast for 15 minutes, or until the fruit is tender and the juices are bubbling, then uncover and give it all a good stir. Continue to roast for 5 or so more minutes, until sticky, slightly caramelized, and reduced. Remove and cool completely.

For the buttercream, put the egg whites and sugar into the bowl of a stand mixer. Set it over a saucepan that's filled with a few inches of barely simmering water. Do not let the base of the bowl touch the water below. Heat, stirring often, until it reaches 160°F (71°C). The sugar will have dissolved and the mixture will be sticky-hot to the touch. Set onto the stand

the sixth sense

In pastry, we're often taught that our creations must make sense. The first signs are visual, achieved by incorporating an element of the dessert's internal flavor into how it looks on the outside; like a fruit, flower, or artistic flair, that informs the eater of what will be experienced. Sometimes I indulge in these tenets, others, I don't. But it is useful for cake decoration. I like to highlight what's inside by reserving roasted rhubarb or its syrup for the top, and roses too. Overt or discreet, how you finish this is personal.

mixer and fit with the whisk attachment. Whisk on medium-high speed until thick and glossy, about 7 minutes. Switch out the whisk for the paddle attachment, then beat in the butter, a tablespoon at a time, waiting until fully blended before adding the next. Beat in the crème fraîche and rose water. Continue to beat until a silky-smooth buttercream has formed.

Set a cake layer onto a serving plate, cut side facing up. Spread over a few tablespoons of the buttercream with an offset palette knife. Slightly indent the middle to create a lip around the edge, which will help to seal in the fruit. Spoon in half of the rhubarb. Press on a second cake layer, cut side facing down. Again, frost and fill, then add on the final layer. Coat the entire cake with the remaining buttercream.

Decorate as desired, then serve. This cake is best eaten on the day of making, and once cut should be loosely covered and refrigerated, up to 5 days. Return to room temperature before eating.

Buckwheat Crêpes and Cream

Sourness can seem like a sensory assault, though how it's harnessed makes all the difference. Here, I lean into the softer side of it. These crêpes operate within a lost zeitgeist, between the leavened blini that I remember from my childhood and the wafer-thin crêpes that I found in France as an adult. Fill these up until they burst, serving with highly strung tart fruits.

/ *Makes about 8 crêpes* /

FOR THE BUCKWHEAT CREAM

½ cup (85 g) raw buckwheat groats

2 cups (480 ml) heavy cream

1 tablespoon confectioners' sugar

Seeds scraped from 1 vanilla bean

FOR THE CRÊPES

1½ cups (360 ml) whole milk

¼ cup (60 g) unsalted butter, cubed

¾ cup (90 g) buckwheat flour

½ cup (60 g) all-purpose flour

¼ cup (50 g) granulated sugar

3 large eggs

1 tablespoon vodka, optional

Cultured butter, for cooking the crêpes

Confectioners' sugar, for finishing

START the buckwheat cream. Preheat the oven to 350°F (180°C). Line a baking sheet with parchment paper, then scatter the groats over it into an even layer. Toast for 10 to 12 minutes, until deeply fragrant. Cool, then tip into a bowl. Stir in 1 cup (240 ml) of the cream. Cover with plastic wrap and leave to infuse in the refrigerator for at least 6 hours, but preferably overnight.

For the crêpes, in a medium saucepan, bring the milk and butter to a simmer over a gentle heat, stirring often, until melted. Remove and set aside. Sift the flours into a large mixing bowl, then stir in the granulated sugar. Make a well in the center, then stream in the warm milk mixture, whisking concentrically until smooth. Whisk in the eggs and vodka, if using. Cover and leave to rest on the kitchen counter for an hour.

When you're ready to fry, set a 10-inch (25-cm) skillet over medium heat. Add in a pat of butter, swirling it around until melted and beginning to brown. Pour in ⅓ cup batter, raising and swirling the pan as you pour, so that a thin film coats the surface of the pan. Cook the crêpe for 2 to 3 minutes, then flip, and cook for another minute or so on the other side until light golden. Transfer to a plate, then wipe out the pan and re-butter. Repeat this process with the remaining batter.

To finish, strain the infused cream through a fine-mesh sieve into a medium mixing bowl, pressing on the backs of the groats to release any juices. Discard the buckwheat. Add 1 cup (240 ml) of the remaining cream, along with the sugar and vanilla seeds. Whisk to soft but stable peaks.

Divide the cream among the crêpes, rolling tightly to enclose. Finish with a dusting of confectioners' sugar. These are best eaten soon after making, served with tart fruit.

Raspberry Vinegar Tart

This seems like an unusual tart, but it makes sense to the palate. I started using vinegar to protect the fruit I care about, and in this glaze, it features with force. There's burnt butter in the crust too, which has a tinge of bitterness, but also mostly warmth, and works to bolster the creamy yet sharp filling. Seasonal and simple, this tastes ripe.

/ *Serves 8* /

FOR THE CRUST

½ cup + 1 tablespoon (130 g) unsalted butter, cubed

1⅓ cups plus 1 tablespoon (175 g) all-purpose flour

⅓ cup (40 g) confectioners' sugar

¼ teaspoon salt

3 large egg yolks

1 large egg white, lightly beaten, for the wash

FOR THE GLAZE

½ cup (100 g) granulated sugar

2 tablespoons raspberry or red wine vinegar

FOR THE FILLING

1 cup (240 ml) heavy cream

2 tablespoons crème fraîche

1 tablespoon confectioners' sugar

2 cups (250 g) fresh raspberries

FOR the crust, put the butter into a deep saucepan, then set it over medium heat. Stir until melted. Raise the heat to high and continue to cook, swirling often but without stirring, until a nutty brown liquid has formed. It will foam, hiss, and crackle, but subside as it nears done. Transfer into a small heatproof bowl, along with the burnt bits, then refrigerate until solid. Once solid, scrape it out and onto a cutting board. Chop into cubes that are roughly about ½ inch (1.3 cm) in size. Add into a large mixing bowl, along with the flour, confectioners' sugar, and salt.

Using your fingers, the blade of a metal spatula, or a combination of both, work the ingredients together to form a sandy and pebble-like mixture. Stir in the yolks with a wooden spoon. Gather the dough into a ball. If you pinch it, it should hold. Pat into a disc, then cover with plastic wrap, and chill for at least an hour, or up to 3 days.

Set a 9-inch (23-cm) fluted tart tin onto a baking sheet. Flour your work surface, then set the dough onto it, lightly dusting the top to prevent sticking. Roll into a rough circle that's a few inches larger than the tin you're using, focusing the concentration of your pressure in the middle then working outward until it's ¼ inch (.6 cm) thick. Fit into the tin—it'll be fragile, so move with precision. Trim off the excess. Freeze, while the oven preheats to 325°F (160°C).

Line the crust with a few layers of parchment paper, then fill it to the brim with ceramic weights or dried beans. Bake for 20 minutes, or until dry and set, then remove and leave to cool slightly. Discard the weights and paper, then reduce the temperature to 300°F (150°C). Prick the base of the tart a few times with a fork and thinly brush over the egg white. Return to the oven and continue to bake for another 15 minutes, until golden. Cool on a wire rack.

Meanwhile, make the glaze. Put the sugar and vinegar into a small saucepan, along with ¼ cup (60 ml) water. Bring to a boil over medium heat, stirring often to dissolve the granules. Remove and cool completely.

the sixth sense

So much of this tart depends on the ripeness of the fruit, and each time I make it, it ends differently. When raspberries don't quite cut it, other jewel-toned fruits like red currants, gooseberries, and cherries are strong contenders, but always, the sourness should remain.

When you're ready to assemble, in the bowl of a stand mixer that's fitted with the whisk attachment, whip the cream, crème fraîche, and confectioners' sugar to soft peaks on medium speed. Place the crust on a serving plate, then add in the whipped cream, swirling it out with the back of a spoon. Arrange over the raspberries, as rough or ornate as desired. Glaze until glistening.

Serve chilled. It'll keep, loosely covered, in the refrigerator for 2 to 3 days.

Linzer Torte

FOR THE PASTRY

1 cup + 1 tablespoon (150 g) ground hazelnuts

2 cups (250 g) all-purpose flour

½ teaspoon baking powder

A dash of ground cinnamon, cloves, and allspice

A pinch of salt

¾ cup (150 g) granulated sugar

¾ cup + 2 tablespoons (200 g) unsalted butter, cold and cut into ½-inch (1.3-cm) cubes

2 large eggs

1 large egg yolk

FOR THE FILLING

2½ cups (800 g) jam, like raspberry, cherry, plum, or red currant

1 tablespoon brandy, optional

Confectioners' sugar, to finish

Though traditionally filled with red currant jam, the level of sour in this recipe is left to you. The pastry is short, sweet, and tender, and it really does not like to be handled. It'll demand some posturing between the freezer and bench, more so if the weather is warm. And this very much is a dessert destined for summer. It gets better the longer it sits, the filling melding into the textural crumb. Fable says three days max—if you can wait that long. I often can't.

/ *Serves 8* /

Adjust a rack to the middle of the oven, then preheat it to 350°F (180°C).

Scatter the hazelnuts into an even layer across a lined baking sheet and roast for 8 to 10 minutes, until deeply golden brown and fragrant. Cool completely, then grind to a meal in a food processor. Transfer into a large mixing bowl, along with the flour, baking powder, cinnamon, cloves, allspice, and salt. Stir in the sugar.

Add the butter into the bowl. With a pastry blender or metal spatula, begin to cut the cubes into the dry ingredients until pebble-sized clumps have formed. Add the eggs and yolk. Stir with a wooden spoon to combine, then bring the dough together into a taut ball. Divide into halves, one a little heftier than the other. Pat each into a disc, then cover with plastic wrap. Chill for at least 2 hours.

Set a 10-inch (25-cm) tart tin that's about 1½ inches (3.5 cm) deep with a removable base onto a baking sheet. Stir together the jam and brandy, if using, to loosen.

Remove the larger dough portion from the refrigerator and position it between two sheets of parchment paper. With a wooden pin, roll it into a rough ⅛-inch (.3-cm) thick circle. Flour and adjust the paper as necessary to avoid creasing, sticking, and tearing. Carefully transfer and fit—it'll be quite tender—then neaten off the excess overhang. Spoon in the jam mixture, smoothing it out evenly over the base.

Roll out the remaining pastry in the same manner as above, though an inch smaller. Slide it onto a baking sheet and freeze until firm. Once frozen, with a sharp knife and working fast, slice it into five 1½-inch (4-cm) wide strips. Lattice, tentatively, over the tart. Pinch or crimp the edges to seal, flouring if it gets too sticky. Freeze the tart while the oven preheats to 350°F (180°C).

Bake for 45 to 50 minutes, until golden brown and bubbling. Transfer to a wire rack to cool completely before carefully unmolding.

Dust the tart with confectioners' sugar before serving. This will keep, sealed in an airtight container, in a cool, dark place for about a week.

Rhubarb Bread Pudding

FOR THE RHUBARB

8 ounces (230 g) rhubarb, washed, trimmed, and cut into finger-sized lengths

¼ cup (60 ml) gin

Juice from 1 orange

2 tablespoons granulated sugar

FOR THE CUSTARD

¼ cup (60 g) unsalted butter, softened, plus more for greasing the dish

Raw sugar, for sprinkling

1½ cups (360 ml) whole milk

1½ cups (360 ml) heavy cream

1 sprig of rosemary

1 cinnamon stick

A thick strip of orange peel

1 pound (450 g) rye sourdough bread, cut into ½-inch (1.3-cm) thick slices

½ cup (85 g) chopped dark chocolate

6 large eggs

¾ cup (150 g) granulated sugar

1 teaspoon vanilla extract

Not built sweet or weak, but weathered and strong, this recipe is for the harsher months. The only intermissions of light inside are sour, and though I am often swept away by such impressions, the thing that warms the most is the herbaceous infused milk that unites all. Rye bread isn't traditional, so if you like a softer and more custardy pudding, use an enriched bread like brioche or challah instead.

/ *Serves 6* /

ADJUST a rack to the middle of the oven, then preheat it to 350°F (180C°).

Place the rhubarb in a single layer into a ceramic baking dish, then pour over the gin and orange juice. Scatter in the sugar. Roast for 15 to 20 minutes, agitating halfway through, until tender. Remove and leave to cool.

Generously grease the bottom and sides of a 4-cup (1-L) capacity ovenproof dish with butter, scattering over enough raw sugar to coat. Bring the milk, cream, rosemary, cinnamon, and peel to a simmer in a large saucepan that's set over medium heat. Set aside to steep.

Next, lightly butter the bread, then halve it. Overlap the slices into the prepared dish, then distribute the roasted rhubarb and chocolate between each fold.

In a large mixing bowl, whisk together the eggs, granulated sugar, and vanilla. Set a fine-mesh sieve over the top and stream in the infused liquid, discarding the aromatics, then whisk softly to combine. Pour over the bread, prying the slices apart so that all of the tight crevices are reached. Scatter with a pinch of more raw sugar. Tent the top with aluminum foil.

Bake for about an hour, uncovering close to the end, until golden, bubbling, and just set. Serve the pudding warm, or close to it. This is best eaten on the day of making, but leftovers can be refrigerated for up to 2 days. Reheat slightly, for its best.

the sixth sense

To highlight and contrast, serve with vanilla ice cream, for the perfect combination of sweet and sour, hot and cold, soft and harsh.

Kefir Fraisier

FOR THE CRÈME PÂTISSIÈRE

1¼ cups (300 ml) whole milk

1 cup (240 ml) kefir

⅔ cup (135 g) granulated sugar

6 large egg yolks

⅓ cup + 1 tablespoon (50 g) cornstarch

2 tablespoons unsalted butter, softened at room temperature

FOR THE SPONGE

1 teaspoon green cardamom pods

4 large eggs

⅔ cup (135 g) granulated sugar

¾ cup + 2 tablespoons (110 g) all-purpose flour

FOR THE SYRUP

¾ cup (150 g) granulated sugar

Juice from ½ a lemon

1 tablespoon fernet, optional

FOR ASSEMBLY

⅔ cup (150 g) unsalted butter, softened at room temperature

1 teaspoon vanilla bean paste

2 cups (300 g) strawberries, washed

FOR THE SUGAR

½ cup (60 g) confectioners' sugar

¼ cup (5 g) freeze-dried strawberries

Nothing is sweeter than strawberries and cream, but for a girl of Russian culture, it's kefir instead. The fermented milk is haunting, strikingly tangy on the nose and palate, and laden with meaning: it was used to treat the sick, the grains were passed down like an heirloom, it became currency, and, like Champagne, it signifies triumph, wealth, and health. Heat kills it, but that's fine, because in this cake, it's not the good bacteria I want—it's the sourness.

/ *Serves 8* /

First, make the crème pâtissière. Pour the milk and kefir into a medium saucepan. Bring to a simmer over gentle heat. Meanwhile, in a medium heatproof bowl, whisk together the sugar, egg yolks, and cornstarch. At this point, the liquid should be warm and soured, with globules that'll split and seem as if they'll never reconcile—they will. Stream into the bowl with the yolks, whisking until combined. Pour it all back into the pan and set on the stove. Continue to heat, whisking continuously until smooth, thick, and glossy. Remove and whisk in the butter. Scrape into a medium heatproof bowl, then cover the surface with plastic wrap. Chill thoroughly.

Adjust a rack to the middle of the oven, then preheat it to 350°F (180°C). Grease and line an 8-inch (20-cm) round springform cake pan with parchment paper, collaring it high.

Make the sponge. Put the cardamom into a dry skillet. Toast over medium heat, shaking often, until tinged a faded olive green. Crack the pods, then extract the seeds and transfer into a mortar and pestle or spice grinder. Grind finely.

Next, put the eggs and sugar into the bowl of a stand mixer. Whisk to incorporate, then set it over a saucepan that's filled with a few inches of barely simmering water. Do not let the base of the bowl touch the water below. Heat over medium heat, whisking often, until it reaches 120°F (50°C) on a thermometer. Remove the bowl and set it onto the mixer. Whisk on high speed until pale, thick, and tripled in volume, about 5 minutes. Sift in the flour and cardamom. Fold until just combined, being cautious not to lose too much air. Scrape into the prepared pan.

(*cont.*)

Bake for 22 to 25 minutes, until golden, springy, and beginning to pull away from the sides of the pan. A skewer inserted into the middle should come out clean. Transfer to a wire rack and leave to cool completely in the pan.

For the syrup, stir together the sugar, lemon juice, and ⅔ cup (160 ml) water in a medium saucepan. Bring to a boil over gentle heat, then remove and stir in the fernet, if using. Cool before use.

When you're ready to assemble the cake, take the same ring that you used to bake, clean it off, and position it onto a serving plate. Line the inside with acetate or parchment paper, a few inches higher than the mold that you're using.

Put the butter into the bowl of a stand mixer that's fitted with the paddle attachment. Beat on medium-high speed for a minute or so until smooth and malleable. Pause to scrape down the bowl, then lower the speed. Beat in the crème pâtissière a third at a time, followed by the vanilla bean paste, until well combined. Switch out the paddle for the whisk attachment. Whisk for 5 or so minutes, until a velvet-like mousseline has formed. Because you're aiming to homogenize two components that are temperature sensitive, it might seize. To rectify, set the bowl over a saucepan of barely simmering water. Warm it up a little, then re-whisk until all of the disparate bits have immersed and the mousseline is luscious once more.

With a sharp serrated knife, slice the sponge horizontally in half. Place the bottom inside the ring, cut side facing up, and soak it with syrup. Halve the strawberries, then trim a little off their sides, to flatten and expose the deep red and white flesh. Arrange over the sponge to form an outer protective edge. Chop the remaining strawberries, then set aside for filling.

Spoon in half of the mousseline, smoothing it out and into the crevices with an offset palette knife. Add the chopped strawberries into the middle, then cover with the remaining mousseline. Soak the sponge for the top and then press it on, cut side facing down. Cover the cake with plastic wrap. Chill until firm, at least 4 hours.

When you're ready to serve, blitz the confectioners' sugar and freeze-dried strawberries to a fine dust in a spice grinder or food processor. Unmold the cake and sift over the vibrant sugar. Adorn with more fresh strawberries, if desired.

This is best eaten on the day of making, and can be kept covered in the refrigerator for up to 3 days. Serve slightly chilled, or close to it.

Passion Fruit Flan

FOR THE CARAMEL

1½ cups (300 g) granulated sugar

⅓ cup + 2 teaspoons (90 ml) passion fruit nectar

FOR THE CUSTARD

2 cups + 2 tablespoons (510 ml) whole milk

1 bay leaf

1 cup (240 ml) heavy cream

3 large eggs

5 large egg yolks

⅓ cup (70 g) granulated sugar

1 teaspoon vanilla extract

Fresh passion fruit pulp, to finish

The starkness of a custard flan was made to be overborne. I do it with passion fruit, which imparts an exotic, citric, and fragrant feel to the dessert, as well as a lot of sourness. It's an effortless way to end a meal and speaks deeply of seasonality. The passion fruit nectar should be taken straight from the fresh fruit, straining out the seeds and extracting the liquid.

/ *Serves 8* /

SET a 9 x 5½-inch (23 x 13-cm) loaf pan in a deep roasting dish.

To make the caramel, put the sugar, nectar, and 2 tablespoons water into a deep saucepan. Stir to incorporate, then bring to a boil over medium heat. Raise the heat to high and continue to cook, swirling occasionally and watching it closely as the liquid tends to froth, until dark golden, like caramel, about 7 minutes. Immediately pour into the prepared pan and stand until hard.

Meanwhile, for the custard, put the milk and bay leaf into a large saucepan. Bring to a simmer over medium heat, then remove. Leave to infuse for half an hour.

Adjust a rack to the middle of the oven, then preheat it to 300°F (150°C). Bring a kettle of water to a boil.

Pour the infused milk into a large mixing bowl, discarding the bay leaf, then stir in the cream. In a separate large bowl, whisk together the eggs, yolks, sugar, and vanilla. Slowly stream in the milk mixture, whisking until combined. Strain through a fine-mesh sieve into the prepared pan, skimming any froth that forms across the top. Pour enough boiling water into the roasting dish so that it reaches halfway up the sides. Tent with aluminum foil.

Bake for 1½ hours, or until just set. The middle of the flan should still retain a wobble. Lift out from the water bath and cool to room temperature, then chill thoroughly, at least 8 hours, but preferably overnight.

When you're ready to serve, position the pan into a few inches of hot water to help melt the caramel top. Run a knife around the edges to loosen the flan, then invert it out and onto a rimmed plate, letting it sit under some pressure until released. Unmold. Adorn with pulp, and serve, with extra spoonfuls of caramel. This keeps in the refrigerator and is best eaten within 2 days.

the sixth sense

This is a classic, old-world dinner-party dessert. To complement it, Madeira or sherry, or a late harvest, like one that's made from Gewürztraminer. Sometimes I'll even slip some orange blossom water into the custard base to increase the aromatic allure.

Preserved Lemon Pie

FOR THE FILLING

About 4 (400 g) lemons

1¾ cups (350 g) granulated sugar

2 tablespoons finely chopped preserved lemon

4 large eggs

¼ teaspoon salt

2 tablespoons unsalted butter, melted

FOR THE CRUST

½ cup (120 ml) ice water

2 teaspoons apple cider vinegar

2¾ cups (345 g) all-purpose flour

½ teaspoon salt

1 cup + 1 tablespoon (245 g) unsalted butter, cold and cut into ½-inch (1.3-cm) cubes

1 egg, lightly beaten, for the wash

Granulated sugar, for finishing

This would be a wound-up pie without a lot of sweetness to release it. The filling is made with a bright composite of lemons—whole and preserved—that are sliced paper thin and left to macerate overnight. During that interlude, sugar and time work together to destabilize the fruit, softening the peel, the pith, the membrane, and de-souring it all, slightly. The next morning the mixture is like confit, and ready to be transformed into pie.

/ *Serves 8* /

The night before you plan to bake, start the filling. Cut the lemons in half, discarding the seeds. Transfer the fruit to the freezer and freeze for an hour or so, until firm. Shave ultra-thin, skin, flesh, and all, with a knife, mandoline, or combination of both. It doesn't have to be perfect—the point is just to get them as fine as possible. Fish out any seeds. If you miss a few, that's fine. They tend to rise to the surface in the morning, so you can extract them then. Place the slices into a large bowl, then add the sugar and preserved lemon. Toss well, then cover with plastic wrap and rest on the kitchen counter overnight.

To make the crust, stir the ice water and vinegar together in a small bowl or measuring cup. Keep cold until needed. Next, put the flour and salt into a large mixing bowl. Add the butter and toss to coat. With the aid of a pastry blender or metal spatula, cut the cubes into the dry ingredients until mostly pebble-sized pieces remain. Drizzle in a few tablespoons of the ice water mixture and stir to incorporate. Continue to add it in, a little at a time, until the dough holds when pinched and squeezed. Some dry flaky bits should remain. Bring together into a ball, then halve and shape each into a disc. Cover with plastic wrap and chill for at least an hour.

Set a 9-inch (23-cm) pie dish onto a rimmed baking sheet. Unwrap the dough onto a floured work surface and dust the tops. Roll into circles that are about ⅛ inch (.3 cm) thick. Fit one into the dish and transfer the other onto a lined baking sheet, which later will be used to form the top crust. Place in the refrigerator while you finish the filling.

Adjust a rack to the middle of the oven, and preheat it to 400°F (200°C).

In a large bowl, whisk together the eggs and salt. Stir in the macerated

(*cont.*)

lemon mixture, along with the melted butter. Pour the filling into the base of the pie. Drape the reserved dough over the top, then trim an inch off the excess overhang. Flute or crimp to seal. Brush it with egg wash and sprinkle with a pinch of sugar. Slit a vent in the middle.

Bake for 45 to 50 minutes, rotating halfway through, until golden brown. Transfer to a wire rack and cool at room temperature, at least 2 hours.

Serve the pie with cream, soured or not. This is best eaten on the day of making. Keep leftovers covered in the refrigerator for 2 to 3 days.

the sixth sense

It's often posited that the sort of lemon used for this pie matters, and a thin-skinned aromatic kind, like Meyer, is preferable. While I do believe that to be true, traditionally this recipe has been made with ordinary table lemons, and though they're not exactly sweet or lovable, I'm not sure if that's the point here.

USED BUT NOT
BROKEN
SO 180
HERITAGE

Cavernous Black Cocoa Cake

FOR THE CAKE

3 large eggs

6 large egg yolks

½ cup + 2 tablespoons (125 g) granulated sugar

⅓ cup + 1 teaspoon (80 ml) olive oil

½ cup (65 g) all-purpose flour

⅓ cup + 2 tablespoons (35 g) Carbon Black or Dutch processed cocoa powder

A pinch of salt

FOR THE CREAM

¾ cup (180 ml) heavy cream

⅓ cup (80 g) crème fraîche

1 tablespoon confectioners' sugar

There's a bit of magic to this cake. Taking divine influence from pão de ló, a Portuguese sponge cake, my version is somewhat sacrilegious from the addition of Carbon Black, a bitter, rich, and deeply pigmented cocoa powder—but don't let that stop you.

Dark, formless, and sunken, the cake should rise, then fall as it cools, resulting in something that's more fondant than cake, but nonetheless delicious. A slightly soured cream is then pushed into the core, bringing it back into lightness and balance. Charmed, I like to serve it in the pan and parchment it was created in.

/ *Serves 6 to 8* /

ADJUST a rack to the middle of the oven, then preheat it to 425°F (220°C). Line an 8-inch (20-cm) round cake pan with a few layers of parchment paper, fluting them in so they overlap and pleat up the sides.

For the cake, in the bowl of a stand mixer that's fitted with the whisk attachment, whisk the eggs, yolks, and sugar on high speed until pale, thick, and tripled in volume, about 5 minutes. The mixture should flow softly back onto itself in a ribbon-like trail when the whisk is raised. Lower the speed and stream in the olive oil, whisking until incorporated. Remove the bowl and sift over the flour, cocoa, and salt. Fold until just combined. Usually, there's a stubborn pocket of dry ingredients hidden somewhere throughout—find it and dig it out.

Bake for 12 to 13 minutes. You want it to be just set but wobbly beneath. Transfer to a wire rack and cool in the pan for 4 to 5 hours, during which time the cake should contract and collapse.

When you're ready to serve, in the bowl of a stand mixer that's fitted with the whisk attachment, whip the cream, crème fraîche, and confectioners' sugar to soft peaks on medium speed. Spoon into the cake's cavity and eat straight after.

Mandarin Sorbetto

About 3 large (315 g) mandarins

1 cup (200 g) granulated sugar

¼ cup (85 g) glucose syrup

¼ teaspoon ground cardamom

A pinch of cracked black pepper

A few saffron threads

3 cups (720 ml) freshly squeezed juice from about 24 mandarins

A pinch of salt

2 tablespoons amaro, optional

I navigate my relationships based on the restaurants we eat at. The most potent belong to the places I return to. Do I want the food or do I want to remember? I ask a vague question to avoid a telling statement.

A sorbetto is tougher than ice cream and icier than sorbet. The constitution of it is sour, but there's a hidden heat that radiates. I could give credit to the spices or amaro, or the favorite Italian place that inspired the recipe, but I think it comes from the mandarin skin. The whole of the fruit is used, not just the juice, like you can sense where the sun has touched it. It tastes nothing like what I remember, and instead a movement toward something greater, finally, a haven.

/ *Serves 6* /

Cut the mandarins into quarters and toss them into a stockpot, along with the sugar, glucose syrup, cardamom, pepper, saffron, and 1 cup (240 ml) of the juice. Bring to a boil over medium heat, then reduce to a simmer. Continue to gently heat until the fruit has softened, swollen, and slumped. Transfer into a blender.

Starting on the lowest speed and increasing as it combines, whir until thin but also pulp-like. Add the salt. Pour into a large bowl or pitcher and stir in the remaining juice and amaro, if using. Cover and chill overnight.

The next morning, set a container or aluminum loaf pan into the freezer. Transfer the sorbetto base into an ice cream machine. Churn according to the manufacturer's instructions. It should be thick and aerated, yet pliant, when done. Quickly extract into the par-frozen container and cover with aluminum foil. Freeze for a few hours, until firm, before serving. This will keep, covered, in the coldest part of the freezer for about 2 weeks.

Salt

Salt is a sensitive word. It comes to the table washed in water and bathed in light, sating not just a bodily need, but also a vibrational one. It tightens, it releases, it cures, and brings everything to the surface, whether we're willing to sink, or swim, or not. ¶ We turn to salt to heal. A flourish can exist as a small act of faith, like a plea or a prayer to some greater power that I don't know the name of but have always heard and understood. My memories of salt are taken from the shore. Young, licking the dried crust off mangrove leaves, then older, subjected to the strange smells of fishing villages in full sun, on the back of my father's motorbike, and then even older, with men, who deliver the line, "I should live in salt." ¶ Experience informs taste, or vice versa, and salt stimulates our innate ability to sense and then receive sugar—through harshness, sweet gets sweeter. Its temperament will endure long after it has been swallowed, meaning it absorbs, and in that dissolution, salt forms part of you. But no fear is needed, as the body was built to take it. ¶ Like water that slips through the fingertips, natural, fleeing, and wild, my approach is never to tame salt, but to steer its spirit, gently. I am of the impression that I'm not in control here, nor do I want to be, for I know that there are limits to love, which cannot be forced but only felt. ¶ Salt should be omnipresent in the construction of dessert, accessible in the shallows yet still lurking in the depths below. A final flourish to finish a cookie or tart shouldn't just taste like the end, or as we so often like to think. But for all that it creates, salt can also destroy. It can destabilize, unbalance, and erode into a space where the palate goes to disintegrate. The precipice is fine, but there, and personal. A lot of these recipes then will not call for a final measurement, as I believe it lives in your lining. Mine, awash with the saline traces of people and places, as ingrained in my skin as a callus, that grew over and over itself, never healing the original wound but just lightly covering it, and that eventually, with enough sweetness, others can touch.

Hot Dip Cookies

FOR THE COOKIES

2¼ cups (280 g) all-purpose flour

⅔ cup + 1 tablespoon (55 g) Dutch processed cocoa powder

1¼ teaspoons baking soda

½ teaspoon salt

¾ cup + 3 tablespoons (215 g) unsalted butter, softened at room temperature

1½ cups (300 g) granulated sugar

1 large egg

1 large egg yolk

1 teaspoon vanilla extract

¼ cup (85 g) molasses

FOR SANDING

½ cup (100 g) granulated sugar

2 teaspoons flaky sea salt

FOR THE GANACHE

1½ cups (300 ml) heavy cream

¾ cup + 1 tablespoon (140 g) finely chopped dark chocolate

1 tablespoon bourbon, optional

Often the best parts of a cookie are those warm, molten moments. But chocolate, stubborn and fastidious, must have its setting point. I replicate how I like it with a ganache dip, which replaces actual chocolate chunks throughout the dough. These salt-cracked cookies are the ideal vessel to submerge, resulting in a collision of crunchy and creamy, salty and sweet.

/ *Makes 20 cookies* /

ADJUST racks to the top, middle, and bottom thirds of the oven, then preheat it to 350°F (180°C). Line three baking sheets with parchment paper.

Sift the flour, cocoa powder, baking soda, and salt into a medium mixing bowl.

In the bowl of a stand mixer that's fitted with the paddle attachment, or using handheld electric beaters, beat the butter and sugar on medium speed until light and fluffy, about 3 minutes. Pause to scrape down the bowl, then beat in the egg, yolk, and vanilla until well combined. Beat in the molasses. The mixture should be creamy and caramel in color. Lower the speed, then tip in the dry ingredients. Beat to form a uniform dough.

Next, for sanding, stir together the sugar and flaky sea salt. Using a generous tablespoon as a scoop, portion the dough into 1½-ounce (45-g) amounts. Roll into smooth balls with the palm of your hands, then rattle in the sanding mixture. Divide among the prepared sheets, leaving a few inches of space apart for spreading.

Bake for 12 to 14 minutes, rotating halfway through, until crackled. The middles should be slightly soft and the edges crisp. Cool for a few minutes on the sheets, then lift the cookies off and onto a wire rack to cool further.

For the ganache, pour the cream into a medium saucepan, then set it over gentle heat. Put the chocolate into a medium heatproof bowl. As soon as the cream has come to a simmer, stream it all over the chocolate. Stand for a minute, then stir until smooth. Stir in the bourbon, if using.

Dip the cookies into the warm ganache, eating soon after. They'll keep, stored in airtight container, at room temperature for 3 days, but the ganache should always be served fresh.

Salted Yolk Custard Tart

FOR THE SALTED YOLKS

Table salt

3 large eggs

FOR THE CRUST

1½ cups (190 g) all-purpose flour

½ cup (60 g) confectioners' sugar

⅓ cup (30 g) ground almonds

A pinch of salt

½ cup (1 stick/115 g) unsalted butter, cold and cut into ½-inch (1.3-cm) cubes

3 large egg yolks

1 large egg, lightly whisked with 1 teaspoon whole milk

FOR THE FILLING

3 cups (720 ml) heavy cream

1 vanilla bean, split

A pinch of grated nutmeg

12 large egg yolks

⅔ cup (135 g) granulated sugar

A lot of my story I had to rewrite. My Chinese heritage wasn't easily translated; I went out and sought it, am in the process of seeking it. Salted egg yolks are something that I remember from my childhood. I thought they were strange then, and to some extent still do—but they're a delicacy for a reason. It was in my search that I could reframe them into sweetness.

The salted yolks enhance this recipe. They're rich, and you won't need to use all of them to complete the tart, but curing in a large batch is easier than small. Gleaming like iridescent apricots, my salt cure is simplified for someone still learning.

Almost every culture has their version of a custard tart. It's nostalgic, loved, and often made with staple ingredients that are accessible to all.

/ *Serves 8* /

First, start the salted yolks. Pour enough salt into a small but deep dish to form a base layer, then, with the bottom of an egg, puncture three depressions into it, spacing each hole a few inches apart. Separate the eggs, stealing the yolks, and setting the whites aside for another use. Drop the yolks into the cavities. Bury them with more salt, flourishing it on so as not to rupture their fragile structure. Wrap the dish loosely in plastic wrap, then transfer to an undisturbed place in the refrigerator. Cure for at least 1 day, or up to 5.

Tentatively unearth the yolks. They'll have turned somewhat hard, sticky, and gummy. Pat off the excess salt, which will have hardened due to absorbing moisture, then gently rinse each yolk under cold water. Dry on a paper towel. Meanwhile, preheat the oven to 150°F (65°C).

Put the yolks onto a wire rack and set it over a baking sheet. Dry in the oven for about 1½ hours, until firm and opaque. Remove and cool completely. Store in an airtight container in the refrigerator until needed to finish the tart. They're best used within a week, and leftovers are an ideal enhancement to have on hand—for both sweet and savory.

To make the crust, whisk together the flour, confectioners' sugar, ground almonds, and salt in a large mixing bowl. Add the butter and toss to coat. Begin to rub and blend the cubes into the dry ingredients until pebble-sized clumps have formed. Add the yolks and stir with a wooden spoon to combine. Bring the dough together, pinching and patting it into shape, then form into a disc. Cover with plastic wrap and chill in the refrigerator for at least an hour.

Position a 10-inch (25-cm) tart tin that's about 1¼ inches (3.5 cm) deep with a removable base onto a baking sheet. Unwrap the dough onto a floured work surface and lightly dust the top. With a wooden pin, roll it into a circle that's about ⅛ inch (.3 cm) thick, or a few inches larger than the tin you're using. Transfer and fit, then neaten off the excess overhang. Transfer to the freezer while the oven preheats to 350°F (180°C).

Line the par-frozen crust with a sheet of parchment paper, then fill to the brim with ceramic weights or dried beans. Bake for 20 minutes, or until set. Cool slightly, then remove the weights. Brush with egg wash and return to the oven. Continue to bake for another 7 to 10 minutes, until golden. Transfer to a wire rack to cool completely, then lower the temperature to 250°F (120°C).

Next, for the filling, pour the cream into a large saucepan. Scrape in the vanilla seeds, then add the pod and nutmeg. Bring to a simmer over medium heat. Meanwhile, in a large heatproof bowl, whisk together the yolks and sugar. As soon as the cream is at temperature, stream it into the yolk mixture, whisking slowly and continuously until incorporated. Strain through a fine-mesh sieve into the crust, filling it to the brim. Pierce any stray bubbles that may have risen to the surface.

Bake for 50 minutes to an hour, until the custard is set but still retains a slight wobble in the middle. Cool to room temperature on a wire rack.

Unmold the tart and slide it onto a serving plate. Finely grate over the salted yolks, the amount to your taste. Slice it in thick wedges. This is best eaten on the day of making but will keep, loosely covered, in the refrigerator for 2 to 3 days.

You will make a change

Duck Fat Caramel Ice Cream

FOR THE ICE CREAM

2 cups (480 ml) heavy cream

1 cup + 2½ tablespoons (280 ml) whole milk

6 large egg yolks

⅔ cup (135 g) granulated sugar

1 teaspoon vanilla extract

FOR THE CARAMEL

1 cup (240 ml) heavy cream

¼ cup (85 g) glucose syrup

Seeds from 1 vanilla bean

1¼ cups (250 g) granulated sugar

2 tablespoons duck fat

A pinch of flaky sea salt

Duck fat is adored for its animalish salt that's subtle, but not without force. The caramel swirled throughout this ice cream is a greater form of itself for it. Rich, luxurious, and flowing like silk, the amount used is left to your preference. The excess can be refrigerated for a week or so, and is ideal for reinvigorating desserts or, indulgently, licked by the spoonful.

/ *Serves 4* /

For the ice cream, pour the cream and milk into a large heavy-bottomed saucepan. Bring it to a simmer over medium heat. Meanwhile, in a medium heatproof bowl, whisk together the egg yolks, sugar, and vanilla until pale and thick. As soon as the liquid has reached temperature, ladle a little of it into the yolks, whisking to combine. Whisk in another ladle, then pour the mixture back into the pan that's set on the stove. Continue to gently heat, stirring constantly, until it's thick enough to coat the back of a spoon, 5 to 6 more minutes. If you have a thermometer, it should fall within a temperature range of 170°F to 180°F (77°C to 82°C). Strain through a fine-mesh sieve into a large heatproof bowl, then cover with plastic wrap. Chill in the refrigerator for at least 8 hours, but preferably overnight.

Make the caramel a few hours before you plan to churn.

Put the cream, glucose syrup, and vanilla seeds into a medium saucepan. Bring to a simmer, stirring to homogenize. Turn off the heat and set aside. Next, in a separate wide saucepan, combine the sugar with ⅓ cup + 2 teaspoons (90 ml) water. Cook over medium-high heat, stirring often to dissolve the granules. Raise the heat to high and continue to cook, swirling often but without stirring, until the liquid is amber. Immediately remove, then carefully stream it into the cream mixture. Whisk to combine, then whisk in the duck fat and flaky salt. Transfer to a medium heatproof bowl. Set aside to cool, then cover, and chill thoroughly.

When you're ready to churn, place a container or aluminum loaf pan into the freezer to keep cold. Churn the ice cream according to the manufacturer's instructions. It will be thick and voluminous when done. Remove the caramel from the refrigerator and give it a vigorous stir until fluid again. Extract the ice cream into the par-frozen container, layering with swirled spoonfuls of the sauce. Cover with aluminum foil and freeze until firm. This will keep, covered, in the coldest part of the freezer for about 5 days.

Fleur de Sel Fudge Cake

FOR THE CAKE

¼ cup (45 g) finely chopped dark chocolate

½ cup (120 ml) hot coffee

1¼ cups + 1 teaspoon (160 g) all-purpose flour

⅔ cup + 1 tablespoon (55 g) Dutch processed cocoa powder

1 teaspoon baking powder

½ teaspoon baking soda

½ teaspoon salt

1 cup (200 g) granulated sugar

¼ cup (55 g) light brown sugar

2 large eggs

⅓ cup + 2 tablespoons (105 ml) vegetable oil

⅔ cup (160 ml) buttermilk

FOR THE SOAK

3 tablespoons dark rum

FOR THE SLICK

½ cup (100 g) granulated sugar

⅓ cup (25 g) Dutch processed cocoa powder

1 teaspoon coffee powder

FOR THE BUTTERCREAM

4 large egg whites

1½ cups (300 g) granulated sugar

1 cup + 2 tablespoons (260 g) unsalted butter, softened at room temperature

1 teaspoon vanilla extract

A pinch of fleur de sel

Essentially a blank canvas, this cake hides a core of darkness, only to be revealed with slicing later on. It does well to be eaten with hands, and also solemnity, for when the opposing forces of frosting and cake meet, they meld. Harsh/soft, light/dark, sweet/salt, the stark surface should be stained as such.

/ *Serves 12 to 16* /

Adjust a rack to the middle of the oven, then preheat it to 350°F (180°C). Grease and line an 8-inch (20-cm) square cake pan with parchment paper.

To make the cake, place the chocolate into a small bowl, then pour over the coffee. Let it sit for a minute, then stir until dissolved.

Sift the flour, cocoa powder, baking powder, baking soda, and salt into a large mixing bowl. Whisk in the sugars, then form a well in the middle. In a separate medium bowl or pouring jug, stir together the eggs, oil, and buttermilk. Pour into the well and whisk to combine, then whisk in the coffee mixture until a thick and smooth batter has formed. Pour into the prepared pan. Bake for 30 to 35 minutes or until a skewer inserted into the middle comes out clean. Allow to cool for 15 minutes, then turn the cake out onto a wire rack to cool completely. Level an inch off the domed top with a sharp serrated knife, then soak the cake well with rum.

Next, make the slick. Put the sugar, cocoa, and coffee powder into a deep saucepan. Stir in ½ cup (120 ml) water. Bring to a simmer over medium heat, whisking often, then lower and reduce down by about a half—it shouldn't take more than a few minutes. Pour into a heatproof bowl and cool completely before use. It'll thicken as it sits.

To make the buttercream, put the egg whites and sugar into the bowl of a stand mixer. Set it over a saucepan that's filled with a few inches of barely simmering water. Heat, whisking often, until it reaches 160°F (71°C) on a thermometer. The sugar granules will have dissolved and the mixture will be sticky-hot to the touch. Transfer to the mixer and fit with the whisk attachment. Whisk on medium-high speed until a thick and glossy meringue has formed, about 7 minutes. Switch out the whisk for the paddle attachment, then lower the speed to medium. Beat in the butter, a tablespoon at a time, until all incorporated, then beat in the vanilla and fleur de sel. Continue to beat to form a silky buttercream.

Set the cake onto a plate. Frost the top and sides thickly with buttercream, then Pollock the sauce over the starkness. Slice and serve, storing any leftovers in an airtight container in the refrigerator for 3 to 5 days.

Salted Butter Shortbread

1¾ cups + 3 tablespoons (240 g) all-purpose flour

½ cup (60 g) cornstarch

1 cup + 2 teaspoons (240 g) salted cultured butter, softened at room temperature

½ cup + 2 tablespoons (125 g) granulated sugar

2 teaspoons vanilla extract

A pinch of flaky sea salt

The reliance on shortbread is always butter, and they're not created equal. Pure, almost white, with a salt content that's strong and refined is ideal, as in this subtle recipe there's nowhere to hide. A salty-sweet crust sheaths the top, which does most of the outward expression, looking fragile and breakable, like how I'd imagine salt sits on a lake. I praise it for its vulnerability.

/ ***Makes 18 to 22 squares*** /

Adjust a rack to the middle of the oven, then preheat it to 325°F (160°C). Grease and line an 8-inch (20-cm) square baking pan with parchment paper, leaving a sling over the sides.

Sift the flour and cornstarch into a medium bowl.

Put the butter into the bowl of a stand mixer that's fitted with the paddle attachment. Beat for a few minutes on medium-high speed, until pale, slick, and silky—like mayonnaise. Pause to scrape down the bowl, then beat in ⅓ cup + 1 teaspoon (75 g) of the sugar until light and creamy. Beat in the vanilla. Again, pause to scrape, then set the speed to low. Beat in the dry ingredients to form a soft dough. Scrape into the prepared pan, patting it down into an even layer with your fingertips. Flourish with the remaining sugar and flaky salt.

Bake for 30 to 35 minutes, until light golden. Cool on a wire rack until warm to the touch, then score the surface lengthwise into fifths, then diagonally, to form a diamond pattern. Cool in the pan, before tentatively lifting the shortbread out, and serving.

I like to eat these after they've rested for a few hours, as I think the texture is more tender, but if you go for them sooner, that's fine too. They'll keep, stored in an airtight container, in a cool, dark place for 3 to 5 days.

the sixth sense

Sometimes I think, who am I to go against tradition? And then the better part of me thinks, do it. I like to incorporate a handful of additions to disrupt on whim, like roasted almonds or macadamias, even cocoa nibs or caramelized white chocolate chunks, to bolster the bitter and sweet. But never more than a handful.

Caramels

2½ cups (500 g) granulated sugar

1⅔ cups (400 ml) heavy cream

¾ cup + 1 tablespoon (280 g) golden or light corn syrup

⅔ cup (150 g) unsalted butter, cubed

1 tablespoon vanilla bean paste

½ teaspoon ras el hanout, optional

Flaky sea salt

Sticky, sweet, and toothsome, the sole constitution of caramel is a lot of sugar, which also means that salt is needed. All of the ingredients, save the salinity, are heated viciously for a stretch of time, an act that's part sensory descent, as well as escalation. The salt comes in at the last moment to retain its strength, and it hits you in waves.

The sort of salt used will make all the difference. Here, I've listed the classic flaky kind, but this recipe isn't limited to that. Fleur, gray, black, smoked, or infused; each has a unique grit, taste, and finish, but the moisture content is the most important part. A granule will either sit crystalline over the shore or disintegrate, imbuing with time.

/ *Makes about 56 caramels* /

Grease and line an 8-inch (20-cm) square baking pan with parchment paper, leaving a sling over the sides.

In a large and deep heavy-bottomed saucepan, stir together the sugar, cream, golden or light corn syrup, butter, vanilla bean paste, and ras el hanout, if using. Clip a candy thermometer to the side of the pan, then position it over medium heat. Cook, stirring often, until dissolved. Raise the heat to medium-high and continue to cook, without stirring, until the mixture reaches firm ball stage, around 245°F (118°C). It'll bubble, boil, and take some time to get there, but don't abandon it, as it accelerates near done. Turn off the heat, then immediately pour the mixture into the prepared pan. Let it settle for a few minutes, then flourish with flaky salt. Leave to cool at room temperature until set, about 4 to 6 hours.

Carefully lift the caramel slab out and onto a cutting board. Slice it into bite-sized morsels with a warm, sharp knife. I like them about 1 inch (2.5 cm) in size, or 8 squares cut from 7 rows. If desired, wrap in waxed paper. These will keep, stored in a cool, dry place, for 3 to 5 days. In warm weather, they're best refrigerated, keeping for weeks.

Knockoff Beer Nut Cake

FOR THE CAKE

¼ cup (25 g) unsalted peanuts

1½ cups (190 g) all-purpose flour

½ teaspoon baking powder

½ teaspoon salt

¾ cup + 1½ tablespoons (190 g) unsalted butter, softened at room temperature

1 cup (200 g) granulated sugar

½ cup (110 g) light brown sugar

4 large eggs

1 teaspoon vanilla extract

½ cup + 2 teaspoons (130 g) sour cream

FOR THE CARAMEL

½ cup (120 ml) pale ale

1 cup (200 g) granulated sugar

½ cup (120 ml) heavy cream

2½ tablespoons unsalted butter

1 teaspoon flaky sea salt

FOR THE FROSTING

½ cup + 1 teaspoon (120 g) unsalted butter, softened at room temperature

2 cups (240 g) confectioners' sugar, sifted

2 tablespoons heavy cream

1 teaspoon vanilla extract

¼ cup (30 g) beer nuts, pounded rough or fine, for finishing

Whether we like it or not, flavor evokes an emotional response, and a mouthful of this cake coagulates into a dimly lit matrix of dank bars with leather lounges, salt-slicked fingers stuck with peanut seed coats, their shells piled sky-high, like an offering.

I don't believe that salt should ever be the dominant experience—especially in dessert. Here, the saline-stricken elements that comprise this cake, through sugar and time, are transformed into a state of softness and sublimity. Eyes wide open, a slice takes me straight back, though how I see now is different. The night is yours until it isn't—our memories eat with us.

/ *Serves 8* /

Adjust a rack to the middle of the oven, then preheat it to 350°F (180°C). Grease and line a 9 x 5½-inch (23 x 13-cm) loaf pan with parchment paper, leaving a sling over the sides.

Make the cake. In a food processor or spice grinder, pulverize the peanuts to a meal, stopping short of damp clumps. Transfer to a medium mixing bowl, then sift in the flour, baking powder, and salt.

In the bowl of a stand mixer that's fitted with the paddle attachment, or using handheld electric beaters, beat the butter and sugars on medium speed until light caramel in color, 3 to 5 minutes. Pause to scrape down the bowl, then beat in the eggs, one at a time, beating well to incorporate after each addition. Beat in the vanilla, then lower the speed. Beat in half of the dry ingredients until combined, followed by all of the sour cream and then the last of the dry ingredients. Beat to form an aerated batter. Scrape it into the prepared pan, smoothing it out with an offset palette knife.

Bake for just over an hour, until golden. A skewer inserted into the middle should come out clean. Cool in the pan for 15 minutes, then turn out onto a wire rack to cool completely.

To make the caramel, put the ale and sugar into a deep saucepan that's set over medium heat. Bring to a simmer, stirring often to dissolve the granules, then raise the heat to medium-high. Continue to cook, swirling the pan often but without stirring, until an amber-hued liquid has formed. It tends to foam, so keep an eye on it—you might need to manipulate your heat and swirling tactics to prevent an overflow. Remove from the heat, then whisk in the cream, butter, and flaky salt. Transfer to a medium heatproof bowl and cool completely before use.

the sixth sense

To inject lightness back into this cake, incorporate the zest of a whole orange. Rubbing the aromatic skin until it releases its waxy, citric, life-affirming oils has always been the thing that helps bring me back into the moment, and my body.

For the frosting, beat the butter, confectioners' sugar, cream, and vanilla until light and fluffy, then beat in 3 generous tablespoons of the caramel. Coat the cake in thick swoops and swirls and then drizzle it with more caramel, if desired. Adorn with beer nuts. This is best eaten on the day of making but will keep, stored in an airtight container, at room temperature for 2 to 3 days.

Salt, Malt, and Spice Cookies

FOR THE CARAMELIZED PECANS

¾ cup + 1 tablespoon (115 g) pecans

2 tablespoons light brown sugar

1 tablespoon glucose syrup

1 teaspoon ras el hanout

A pinch of flaky sea salt

FOR THE COOKIES

2½ cups (315 g) all-purpose flour

2 tablespoons malted milk powder

½ teaspoon baking soda

¼ teaspoon salt

¾ cup + 1½ tablespoons (190 g) unsalted butter, softened at room temperature

¾ cup + 1 teaspoon (170 g) light brown sugar

⅓ cup (70 g) granulated sugar

1 teaspoon vanilla extract

½ cup (85 g) chopped dark chocolate

Flaky sea salt or smoked salt, to finish

Savory, salty, smoky, and somewhat sweet, these are more of the defiant cookie kind. They aren't chaste to the usual confines of texture or taste, with a good amount of heat from ras el hanout, which ties all of the opposing elements together. I find that they transform greatly in a mouthful. Hard to define or put down, I get the sense that I shouldn't.

/ *Makes 21 cookies* /

First, make the caramelized pecans. Tip the nuts into a dry skillet, then set it over medium-high heat. Toast, shaking often, until fragrant. Add the light brown sugar, glucose syrup, and ras el hanout. Continue to cook for a few more minutes, agitating occasionally, until a dark, sticky, and aromatic caramel has coated the nuts. Immediately scrape the mass out and into a cluster on a lined baking sheet. Season with the flaky salt, and leave to harden. Chop rough.

Next, for the cookies, sift the flour, malted milk powder, baking soda, and salt into a medium mixing bowl.

In the bowl of a stand mixer that's fitted with the paddle attachment, or using handheld electric beaters, beat the butter and sugars on medium speed until pale caramel in color, 3 to 5 minutes. Pause to scrape down the bowl, then beat in the vanilla. Lower the speed, then tip in the dry ingredients and beat until just combined. Beat in the chocolate and pecans until evenly distributed throughout the crumbly dough. Scrape it onto a sheet of plastic wrap, then shape into a taut cylinder that's about 2 inches (5 cm) wide. Cover and chill until firm enough to slice, about an hour.

Adjust racks to the top, middle, and bottom thirds of the oven, then preheat it to 350°F (180°C). Line three baking sheets with parchment paper.

Unwrap the dough and set it onto a cutting board. With a sharp knife, slice it into ¾-inch (2-cm) thick rounds, rotating as you go to ensure that it's kept as round and intact as possible. Divide among the prepared sheets, leaving some space apart. Sprinkle with flaky or smoked salt.

Bake for 12 to 14 minutes, rotating halfway through, until the edges are golden and crisp but the center is still soft. Stand for a few minutes, then transfer the cookies off the sheets and onto a wire rack to cool further. They're good warm and molten, but best after cooling for a few hours, turning somewhat disintegrated. These will keep stored in an airtight container at room temperature for 3 to 5 days.

Deep-Fried Ice Cream

My Chinese grandfather owned a suburban restaurant that did all of the Asian Australian fused classics—deep-fried ice cream was one, and likened to a fable. Golden, crackled, and crisp, the frozen core was coated in a thin layer of cake crumbs, then drenched in caramel. It was brilliant—or so I've been told—he never could make it for me. Though slightly altered, this is how I make mine and go on remembering him.

/ *Serves 4* /

FOR THE DEEP-FRIED ICE CREAM

1 pint (475 g) ice cream

1½ cups (115 g) cornflakes

½ cup + 1 teaspoon (45 g) desiccated coconut

A pinch of salt

2 large eggs

1 large egg yolk

1 tablespoon whole milk

FOR THE SAUCE

1 teaspoon oolong tea leaves

1¼ cups (250 g) granulated sugar

¾ cup (180 ml) heavy cream

2 tablespoons unsalted butter

Flaky sea salt

Vegetable oil, for frying

LINE a baking sheet with parchment paper, setting it near to the space where you're working. Divide the ice cream into four portions. Cover with plastic wrap and, working fast, shape each into smooth balls. Place onto the sheet and freeze until hard, a few hours.

Next, blitz the cornflakes into a fine dust in a food processor or blender. Transfer into a shallow bowl, along with the desiccated coconut and salt. Remove the ice cream balls from the freezer and unwrap them. Quickly roll each in the mixture, packing it on well to cover and stick. Try to keep them as round as possible too. Re-wrap and return to the sheet. Freeze again until very firm.

In a separate bowl, whisk together the eggs, yolk, and milk. Again, remove the balls, but this time, dip them in the egg mixture. Immediately roll in the crunchy mixture for a final, thick coat. Freeze for at least 8 hours or, preferably, overnight.

Just before you're ready to fry, make the sauce. Blitz the oolong tea leaves with half of the sugar to a fine and fragrant powder. Transfer into a medium heavy-bottomed saucepan, along with the rest of the sugar. Pour in ⅓ cup (80 ml) water. Bring to a boil over medium heat, stirring often to dissolve the granules, then raise the heat to medium-high. Continue to cook, swirling the pan often but without stirring, until deep amber in hue. Slide off from the heat and stream in the cream, whisking with caution, then whisk in the butter and flaky salt. Transfer to a medium heatproof bowl.

Pour a few inches of oil into a deep, large saucepan. Attach a thermometer to the side and steadily bring to 375°F (190°C) over medium heat. Working one at a time, fry the frozen balls until golden and crisp, less than a minute. Remove with a slotted spoon onto a paper towel–lined plate to absorb the excess oil, then transfer into serving bowls.

Serve immediately with the sauce and an extra sprinkling of flaky salt.

the sixth sense

This recipe isn't limited to vanilla—all flavors of ice cream would be divine and lead you down a path, devout or not.

Ivoire and Caviar

¾ cup + 2 tablespoons (150 g) finely chopped white chocolate

1¾ cups + 2 tablespoons (450 ml) heavy cream

A thick strip of lemon peel

Caviar

There's a softness to white chocolate that speaks in hushed tones of vanilla and milk, and when paired with salty, rich caviar makes for a strangely natural pairing. Overwhelm is a word often associated with both ingredients, and restraint is needed. The dark pearls create the spine of this dessert; contrasting as well as complementing, they pull all the weight. The white chocolate then should be thoughtfully considered. I like to use Valrhona Ivoire 35%, which is sweet, delicate, and entirely sensual.

/ ***Serves 4*** /

PUT the white chocolate into a medium heatproof bowl, then pour 1¼ cups (300 ml) of the cream into a medium saucepan, along with the lemon peel. Bring to a simmer over gentle heat, then stream it all over the chocolate, withholding the peel. Leave to sit undisturbed for a moment, then stir to form a smooth ganache. Chill until completely cold, a few hours.

Just before you're ready to serve, scrape the ganache into the bowl of a stand mixer that's fitted with the whisk attachment. Pour in the remaining ⅔ cup (150 ml) of cream. Whisk on medium speed until supple peaks have formed.

Serve the whipped cream with the caviar, bumped or adorned over the top, pressing the pearls to the roof of the mouth with your tongue, and letting it melt, then inhaling, for a sense of salt, sweetness, and the sea.

the sixth sense

The female line in my family has its roots in Siberia; home to the mountains, the cold, and also the sturgeon. My grandmother talks a lot about Lake Baikal, and my mother recalls how normal it was to eat caviar as a child without understanding the price until later. That's what I seek to evoke when I make this dessert—the pleasure, but the pain, our shared history. I choose a caviar that allows me to express similar.
I live on an island now, and it's not that easy to access Siberian without a ship, or significant forethought. There are alternatives that, for me, are equally evocative. Choose a caviar that speaks to your sense of place. The stamp and pedigree, I have found, may not always be best.

Black Olive Madeleines

FOR THE MADELEINES

½ cup (65 g) black olives, pitted

¾ cup (95 g) cake flour

½ teaspoon baking powder

½ cup + 1 teaspoon (120 g) unsalted butter, cubed

2 large eggs

½ cup (100 g) granulated sugar

½ teaspoon vanilla bean paste

FOR THE GLAZE

1⅔ cups (200 g) confectioners' sugar, sifted

3 to 4 tablespoons orange juice

I can't claim these entirely. I took inspiration from David Kinch in *Manresa*, which lists a madeleine with olive caramel, and then Will Goldfarb in *Room for Dessert*, who heightens the black flesh with another of its kind, a pulp-like paste made from kluwak, the fermented seeds of once-poisonous fruit, also known as "Truffle of the East." I indulge in these stories. Everything has a root, cause, and origin, and a recipe should speak to the place and hand that created it. For me, these are pure olive, tasting like salt, summer, and the sea. They're best eaten on the day of making or rehydrated with a nip of gin.

/ *Makes 16 madeleines* /

Adjust racks to the top and bottom thirds of the oven, and preheat it to 400°F (200°C). Butter and flour two 8-hole madeleine pans, tap out the excess, then transfer to the freezer.

Next, pulverize the olives to a granular paste in a food chopper or processor. Scrape into a small bowl and set aside until needed.

Sift the cake flour and baking powder into a medium mixing bowl.

Put the butter into a medium saucepan and set it over medium-high heat. Stir until melted. Raise the heat and continue to cook, swirling the pan often but without stirring, until a nutty brown liquid has formed. It will foam, hiss, and crackle, but subside as it nears done. Pour into a small heatproof bowl, scraping in any burnt bits, and leave to cool.

In the bowl of a stand mixer that's fitted with the whisk attachment, whisk the eggs, sugar, and vanilla bean paste on medium-high speed until pale, thick, and voluminous, about 5 minutes. The mixture should softly fall back onto itself in a flowing trail when the whisk is lifted. Fold in the dry ingredients just to the point where large streaks have disappeared, then fold in the burnt butter, followed by the olive paste. Spoon into the frozen cavities, filling them almost to the top.

Bake for 11 to 13 minutes, until golden and springy. Remove, then immediately release the madeleines onto a wire rack. Cool completely.

For the glaze, whisk together the confectioners' sugar and orange juice in a small bowl. It should be viscous, trailing, and smooth—similar to the consistency of pouring cream. Dip in the madeleines, shell side facing down. Return to the rack and let set before serving. Store in an airtight container at room temperature and eat within 3 days.

Salted Chocolate Tartlets

FOR THE PASTRY

2½ cups (315 g) all-purpose flour

¾ cup (90 g) confectioners' sugar

⅔ cup (50 g) Dutch processed cocoa powder

¼ teaspoon salt

¾ cup + 1 tablespoon (185 g) unsalted butter, softened

4 large egg yolks

1 large egg white, whisked with 1 teaspoon water, for the wash

FOR THE FILLING

1½ cups (255 g) chopped dark chocolate

1 cup (2 sticks/230 g) unsalted butter, cubed

6 large eggs

¾ cup (150 g) granulated sugar

2 tablespoons light brown sugar

½ cup (60 g) all-purpose flour

⅓ cup (25 g) Dutch processed cocoa powder

FOR THE GANACHE

¾ cup (130 g) finely chopped dark chocolate

⅔ cup (160 ml) heavy cream

Dutch processed cocoa powder, for finishing

Flaky sea salt, for flourishing

These are petite but pack a punch. Truffle-like, the triple chocolate filling is in true fighting form; slightly sweet but mostly bitter, it threatens to consume all that surrounds it. The salt is what binds the striking elements in this dessert together. It tightens but amplifies, and though the addition is slight, by no means is the final act performed in vain. A flourish is poignant, a sliver of light amid the dark.

/ *Makes 10 tartlets* /

For the pastry, sift together the flour, confectioners' sugar, cocoa powder, and salt into a medium mixing bowl.

In the bowl of a stand mixer that's fitted with the paddle attachment, beat the butter on medium speed for a minute or so until smooth and malleable. Add the egg yolks, one at a time, and beat until combined. Pause to scrape down the bowl, then set the speed to low. Tip in the dry ingredients. Beat until the dough has balled together, then scrape and gather it up. Divide in half, shaping each into a disc. Cover with plastic wrap and chill for an hour.

Position ten 4-inch (10-cm) tartlet tins across two lined baking sheets. Flour your work surface, then set the dough onto it. Divide into ten portions, rolling each into a circle that's about ¼ inch (.6 cm) thick. Fit into the tins and trim off the excess overhang. Freeze, while the oven preheats to 325°F (160°C). Adjust racks to the top and bottom thirds of it.

Line the tartlet shells with parchment paper, filling to the brim with weights or dried beans. Bake for 15 minutes, or until set, then remove and cool slightly. Remove the paper and weights and coat thinly with the egg white wash. Return to the oven. Continue to bake for another 5 minutes, or until dry. Cool on a wire rack while you prepare the filling.

Put the chocolate and butter into a medium heatproof bowl. Set it over a saucepan that's filled with a few inches of barely simmering water. Stir often over gentle heat until melted.

Next, in the bowl of a stand mixer that's fitted with the whisk attachment, whisk the eggs and sugars on medium-high speed until pale, thick, and doubled in volume, about 5 minutes. Lower the speed, then stream in the melted chocolate mixture. Whisk until combined. Sift over the flour and cocoa, folding it in with a tentative touch. Divide among the shells, filling them almost to the top.

Bake for 12 to 14 minutes, until crackled and glossy. Transfer to a wire rack, unmold, and then leave to cool completely.

Meanwhile, make the ganache. Put the chocolate into a medium heatproof bowl and pour the cream into a small saucepan. Bring it to a simmer, then stream all over the chocolate. Stir slowly until smooth. Cover with plastic wrap and refrigerate until firm enough to scoop.

To serve, dust the tartlets with additional cocoa, then warm a teaspoon and spoon over the ganache. Finish with flaky salt. These will keep, covered, in the refrigerator for 3 to 5 days.

the sixth sense

The salt will shift the course of these tartlets significantly, like a butterfly flaps its wings and it's felt across the ocean sort of thing. I use flaky sea salt, or fleur de sel, which is harvested from the thin and delicate crust of seawater. Sel gris is another I often rely on. It's moist and coarse, formed on the bottom layer instead of the top, and it tastes like that too. Be led with your finishing salt, a thing that's so pure and elemental it has no choice but to steer.

Licorice Cake

FOR THE CAKE

Softened unsalted butter, for the pan

½ cup + 1 teaspoon (45 g) Carbon Black cocoa powder, plus more for the pan

⅓ cup (85 g) soft black licorice, finely chopped

1½ cups (190 g) all-purpose flour

1 teaspoon baking soda

½ teaspoon baking powder

¼ teaspoon salt

A pinch of ground star anise

1½ cups (300 g) granulated sugar

2 large eggs

½ cup + 1 tablespoon (135 g) sour cream

½ cup + 1 tablespoon (130 g) unsalted butter, melted

1 teaspoon vanilla extract

FOR THE GLAZE

½ cup + 1 tablespoon (125 g) light brown sugar

¼ cup (60 g) unsalted butter, cubed

¼ cup (60 ml) heavy cream

½ teaspoon vanilla extract

2 teaspoons flaky sea salt

The use of licorice in dessert can induce hesitation. Metallic and sweet with notes of molasses, the black, bitter mass has another world residing beneath the surface. It likes salt, and sometimes comes imbued or coated in it, my favorite to eat. And while this cake comes in Bundt form, without the sweet glaze, it could also be considered savory enough to pass as bread. A bit of salted butter on the side, and that's more than enough.

/ *Serves 8* /

Adjust a rack to the middle of the oven, then preheat it to 350°F (180°C). Generously grease a 5-cup capacity Bundt pan with butter. Dust with cocoa powder, then tap out the excess.

Put the licorice into a medium saucepan, along with 1¼ cups (300 ml) water. Bring to a boil over medium-high heat, then reduce the heat to low. Gently simmer, stirring and smoothing often, until the licorice has dissolved into a sheened charcoal liquid. It will take some time for it to disappear—turn on the music and fall into the rhythm. Top up with more water as needed to prevent the concoction from catching as it reduces.

Transfer to a blender and whir on low speed until homogenized. Pass it through a fine-mesh sieve and into a medium bowl, then re-measure. You'll need 1 cup (240 ml) of the licorice liquid. If you come just under, add in enough hot water to replenish the amount back to the total called for.

Sift the flour, cocoa powder, baking soda, baking powder, salt, and star anise into a large mixing bowl. Stir in the sugar, then push the ingredients aside to form a well in the middle. In a separate bowl, whisk together the eggs, sour cream, butter, and vanilla. Pour into the well, then whisk until thick and smooth. Whisk in a little of the licorice liquid to loosen, then add the rest, whisking, until uniform. Pour into the prepared pan, filling it a few inches from the top.

Bake for 50 minutes to an hour, until a skewer inserted into the middle comes out clean. Remove and leave to cool for 10 minutes, then pry the edges—you don't want the cake ripping or tearing as it comes out. Unmold onto a wire rack and leave to cool completely.

To glaze, put the light brown sugar, butter, cream, and vanilla into a medium saucepan. Bring to a simmer over gentle heat, stirring often, until dissolved. Continue to cook for a few more minutes, until thickened and reduced by about a half. Stir in the flaky salt. Transfer the glaze into a small

heatproof bowl and let it cool to room temperature, stirring often as it sits to help it along.

Set the cake onto a rimmed plate and pour the glaze over the top, concentrating the action in the crevices and then edging it over so that it drips down the sides. Allow to set, and then serve. This is best eaten on the day of making.

Chèvre Cheesecake

FOR THE CRUST

¾ cup + 1½ tablespoons (110 g) graham cracker crumbs

¼ cup (35 g) roasted almonds, finely chopped

1 teaspoon fresh thyme leaves

A pinch of salt

3 tablespoons unsalted butter, melted

FOR THE FILLING

2¼ cups (500 g) cream cheese

⅓ cup (75 g) goat cheese

¾ cup (150 g) granulated sugar

3 large eggs

¾ cup + 2 tablespoons (210 g) heavy cream

the sixth sense

The complexity of goat cheese is complemented by a wealth of ingredients. I like to work with the seasons for this cake. In summer, fruit in varied states of raw to roasted, like plums, cherries, apricots, or strawberries, even figs, and in spring, adorning the top with infused honey or preserved lemon rind. As it cools, things can become more intense but still doing no more than necessary to maintain fragility. A citric dark chocolate, like Valrhona Manjari 64% in a 1:1 ganache makes for an elegant end.

The spectrum of taste that exists inside goat cheese is great, ranging from pleasant, in mineral, citrus, and brine, to soft, dustied, and earthen. Lore tells that how the cheese presents depends on the terroir and treatment of the animal, but at its core there is a striking salinity that works well in rich cheesecake. Use a good French chèvre for this recipe, neutral, and not in oil. I like to eat a slice unadulterated, but it can be too strong for some, so how you finish it is left to the imagination—consult with your sixth sense, or mine.

/ *Serves 8* /

Adjust a rack to the middle of the oven, then preheat it to 350°F (180°). Grease and line an 8-inch (20-cm) round springform cake pan with parchment paper, sheathing it with a few layers of aluminum foil around the outside. Bring a kettle of water to a boil.

For the crust, put the graham cracker crumbs, almonds, thyme, and salt into a medium bowl. Pour in the butter and stir until evenly moistened. Tip the mixture into the prepared pan, and press it into an even layer with the back of a spoon. Bake for 10 to 12 minutes, until golden brown. Cool on a wire rack while you make the filling.

Lower the oven temperature to 250°F (120°C). Pour enough boiling water into a deep roasting dish until it's about halfway full, then set it on the oven floor.

In the bowl of a stand mixer that's fitted with the paddle attachment, or using handheld electric beaters, beat the cream cheese, goat cheese, and sugar for a few minutes on medium speed, until smooth. Pause to scrape down the bowl, then set the speed to low. Beat in the eggs, one at a time, incorporating well after each addition. Slowly stream in the cream, and beat until well combined. Pass the batter through a fine-mesh sieve into the crust, smoothing out any lumps.

Bake for 1¼ hours, or until just set but still with a slight tremble in the middle. Turn off the oven and remove the dish of water. Leave the cheesecake to rest inside with the door propped open until it has returned to room temperature. Transfer to the refrigerator, and chill thoroughly.

To serve, release the cheesecake from the pan and carefully slide it onto a plate, peeling off the paper. Adorn as desired or leave it stark—like a canvas. This will keep, covered, in the refrigerator for 2 to 3 days.

Macaroons

FOR THE MACAROONS

4 large egg whites

1 cup (200 g) granulated sugar

Zest from ½ a makrut lime

2¼ cups (190 g) desiccated coconut

¾ cup (60 g) shredded coconut

¼ teaspoon salt

1 tablespoon rum, optional

FOR THE COATING

¾ cup (130 g) chopped dark chocolate

Flaky sea salt

I have a shuddering need to salt all dessert, and these macaroons are no exception. Their appearance is rough but intricate, and also somewhat thwarted, unassuming to the eye of the flavor that lies inside. I like to use makrut limes to lighten these cookies—but any citrus zest will do. The point is to release alluring aromas into every crevice of desiccated coconut, an ingredient that can sometimes seem like a pile of sawdust if not handled with care. That also comes in the form of slick chocolate and salt—tact.

/ ***Makes 15 macaroons*** /

ADJUST racks to the top and bottom thirds of the oven, then preheat it to 350°F (180°C). Line two baking sheets with parchment paper.

In a wide and heavy-bottomed saucepan, combine the egg whites, sugar, zest, both coconuts, the salt, and rum, if using. Stir continuously with a wooden spoon over medium-low heat until warm, sticky, and thick. It'll seem difficult at first, but will come together as the sugar melts into a gloopy mess. Lower the heat and keep stirring until the mixture has dried out and developed enough resistance to scoop. It should pull and clump as you stir. Slide off from the heat.

With a 2¾-inch (7-cm) scoop or generous tablespoon as a measure, portion out even-sized mounds onto the prepared sheets, leaving a few inches of space apart for spreading.

Bake for 15 to 17 minutes, rotating halfway through, until puffed and tinged deep golden brown. Remove and cool completely on the sheets.

To coat, put the chocolate into a heatproof bowl, then set it over a saucepan that's filled with a few inches of barely simmering water. Do not let the base touch the water below. Stir over medium-low heat until melted.

Dip the macaroons into the chocolate, shaking off the excess and then returning them to the sheets. Slant on their sides, as not to disrupt the coating. Sprinkle with flaky salt. Allow to set before serving.

These will keep, sealed in an airtight container, in a cool, dark place for about a week.

Pretzel Silk Pie

FOR THE CRUST

½ cup (1 stick/115 g) unsalted butter, cubed

5¼ ounces (150 g/about 10) digestive biscuits

2 ounces (55 g) salted pretzels

1 tablespoon granulated sugar

FOR THE FILLING

4 large eggs

¾ cup (150 g) granulated sugar

⅓ cup (70 g) dark brown sugar

¾ cup + 2 tablespoons (150 g) finely chopped dark chocolate

2 teaspoons vanilla extract

1 teaspoon rum, optional

¾ cup (170 g) unsalted butter, softened at room temperature

½ cup (120 ml) heavy cream

FOR THE TOP

½ cup + 2 tablespoons (150 ml) heavy cream

2 tablespoons crème fraîche

FOR THE FRAGMENTS

½ cup (85 g) finely chopped dark chocolate

1 teaspoon coconut oil

Silk pie is a curiosity. True to its name, this silky mousse-like dessert is one that I often find too sweet, though its allure, sitting temptingly from the back of the refrigerator, is far greater than any hesitation I might have. With each step, I aim to counteract the overwhelm of the condensed filling; the pretzel crust designed to offer just enough salt to resist against it. Crisp and disintegrating, it seems hardly stable enough to support weight, but it does, wonderfully.

/ *Serves 8* /

Adjust a rack to the middle of the oven, then preheat it to 350°F (180°C). Position a 9-inch (23-cm) pie plate onto a baking sheet.

To make the crust, put the butter into a saucepan, then set it over medium-high heat. Cook, stirring often, until melted. Raise the heat and continue to cook, swirling occasionally but without stirring, until a nutty brown liquid has formed. It will foam, hiss, and crackle, but subside as it nears done. Transfer into a medium heatproof bowl, along with the burnt bits, and set aside to cool. Meanwhile, blitz the digestive biscuits, pretzels, and sugar in a food processor to a fine crumb. Add into the burnt butter bowl, and stir until evenly moistened. Tip the mixture into the pie plate, pressing to compact it over the base and up the sides. Bake for 12 to 14 minutes, until golden brown. Remove and leave to cool on a wire rack.

For the filling, put the eggs and sugars into a large heatproof bowl. Whisk to combine, then set the bowl over a saucepan that's filled with a few inches of barely simmering water. Whisk slowly over medium heat, until it reaches 160°F (71°C) on a thermometer, about 5 minutes. The mixture should be light like caramel, thick, and aerated. Remove from the heat and add in the chocolate, vanilla, and rum, if using. Whisk until smooth and glossy.

Next, in the bowl of a stand mixer that's fitted with the paddle attachment, beat the butter for a few minutes on medium-high speed until pale, slick, and silky—like mayonnaise. Pause to scrape down the bowl, then lower the speed. Pour in the melted chocolate mixture. Beat to combine, then raise the speed to medium. Continue to beat until mousse-like, 3 to 5 minutes. Set aside while you whip the cream to soft peaks in a separate bowl. Fold both mixtures together, then smooth over the crust. Refrigerate until set, at least 4 hours.

For the top, just before you're ready to serve, whip the cream and crème fraîche to soft peaks in the bowl of a stand mixer that's set on medium speed. Swoop it over the pie. Return to the refrigerator while you make the fragments.

Line a baking sheet with parchment paper. Put the chocolate into a medium heatproof bowl and set it over a saucepan that's filled with a few inches of barely simmering water. Do not let the base of the bowl touch the water below. Stir until melted. Remove and thoroughly stir in the coconut oil. Pour onto the prepared sheet, slicking it out into a thin layer with an offset palette knife. Freeze until solid—it won't take long—then shatter.

Stud the fragments over the pie and serve soon after. This is best eaten on the day of making and can be kept for 2 to 3 days, covered, in the refrigerator.

Kitchen Sink Cookies

2½ cups (315 g) all-purpose flour

1 teaspoon baking powder

¾ teaspoon baking soda

½ teaspoon salt

1 cup + 2 teaspoons (240 g) unsalted butter, softened at room temperature

1 cup (220 g) light brown sugar

½ cup + 1½ tablespoons (120 g) granulated sugar

2 large eggs

2 teaspoons vanilla extract

¾ cup (130 g) chopped dark chocolate

About ½ cup (65 g) additions, like pretzels, potato chips, peanuts, and salted caramel bits, chopped

Flaky sea salt, to finish, optional

Everything but the kitchen sink, the expression joyous in euphemism as well as cookie customization. My favorite, all of the salted things, like pretzels, chips, and peanuts, with caramels and chocolate in between. It wouldn't be a cookie without the chocolate, or salt, and these shouldn't need too much of an additional pinch to finish them off. The inside contains all.

/ ***Makes 22 cookies*** /

WHISK the flour, baking powder, baking soda, and salt in a medium mixing bowl.

In the bowl of a stand mixer that's fitted with the paddle attachment, or using handheld electric beaters, beat the butter and sugars on medium speed until creamy and pale caramel in color, 3 to 5 minutes. Pause to scrape down the bowl, then beat in the eggs, followed by the vanilla. Set the speed to low. Beat in the dry ingredients until just combined, then fold in the chocolate and additions until evenly distributed throughout the dough. Cover with plastic wrap and chill until firm enough to handle, about an hour.

Adjust racks to the top, middle, and bottom thirds of the oven, then preheat it to 350°F (180°C). Line three baking sheets with parchment paper.

With a medium 2¾-inch (7-cm) scoop, portion the chilled dough into even-sized amounts onto the sheets, leaving a few inches of space apart for spreading. You should be able to fit 8-ish per sheet. Flourish with flaky salt, if desired.

Bake for 10 to 12 minutes, rotating halfway through, until the edges of the cookies are crisp but the middles are still soft. Leave to cool on the sheets for a few minutes, then transfer off and onto a wire rack to cool further before serving.

These will keep, stored in an airtight container, at room temperature for 3 to 5 days.

Florentine Bars

FOR THE SHORTBREAD BASE

1½ cups + 1 teaspoon (190 g) all-purpose flour

¼ cup (25 g) ground almonds

½ cup (60 g) confectioners' sugar

½ teaspoon finely chopped fresh rosemary

¼ teaspoon salt

¾ cup (170 g) unsalted butter, melted

FOR THE FILLING

1 cup (200 g) granulated sugar

½ cup (120 ml) heavy cream

½ cup (1 stick/115 g) unsalted butter, cubed

¼ cup (85 g) honey

1 teaspoon vanilla extract

Zest from ½ an orange

2 cups (230 g) flaked almonds

2 tablespoons diced candied citrus peel

Flaky sea salt, for finishing

FOR THE COATING

½ cup (85 g) finely chopped dark chocolate

The history of a Florentine is just as obscure as its long list of ingredients. Some say that it was a Medici chef who started the trend, others, a resemblance to coins or coming from the kitchens of King Louis XIV, again with gilt and another Medici reference, but none go so far as to claim the cookies come from Florence itself.

Crisp, golden, and toffee-like, with nuts, fruit, and sometimes a wave of chocolate, these ingot-like bars are faithful to tradition, while also creating my own. It's a rather butcher-shop amalgamation of what you can include in this recipe. The shortbread base will support.

/ *Makes 12 bars* /

Adjust a rack to the middle of the oven, then preheat it to 350°F (180°C). Grease and line an 8-inch (20-cm) square baking pan with parchment paper, leaving a sling over the sides.

For the base, put the flour, almonds, confectioners' sugar, rosemary, and salt into a medium bowl. Pour in the butter and stir until evenly moistened. Tip into the prepared pan and press the mixture down into a flat layer with your fingertips. Bake for 17 to 20 minutes, until golden. Transfer to a wire rack.

Next, for the filling, put the sugar, cream, butter, honey, vanilla, and zest into a wide and heavy-bottomed saucepan. Stir over medium heat until dissolved, then raise the heat to high and bring the mixture to a boil. Continue to cook without stirring until it reaches 235°F (112°C) on a candy thermometer. Turn off the heat and immediately add the almonds and candied citrus peel. Stir to combine, then scrape the sticky mass over the crust, spreading it out with an offset palette knife. Return to the oven and bake for another 16 to 18 minutes, until golden and bubbling. Stand for 5 minutes or so, then flourish the top with flaky salt. Cool completely.

For the coating, put the chocolate into a medium heatproof bowl that's set over a saucepan filled with a few inches of barely simmering water. Do not let the base of the bowl touch the water below. Stir to melt, then remove. Cool the chocolate on the kitchen counter until it reaches a thick but still pourable consistency. Spoon it over the slab and let set.

When you're ready to serve, lift out and onto a cutting board, running a knife around the edges of the pan to loosen any sticky caramel remnants. Slice horizontally, then lengthwise, into even bars—I think 12 is generous. These can be stored in an airtight container in a cool, dark place for 2 to 3 days.

Saltbush Syrup Cake

FOR THE CAKE

1⅓ cups + 1 teaspoon (140 g) almonds

1¼ cups (160 g) all-purpose flour

1½ teaspoons baking powder

¼ teaspoon salt

1 cup (2 sticks/230 g) unsalted butter, softened at room temperature

1 cup + 1 tablespoon (215 g) granulated sugar

⅓ cup (115 g) honey

Zest from 1 orange

4 large eggs

A handful of flaked almonds, for the top

FOR THE SYRUP

1 teaspoon ground dried saltbush

½ cup (170 g) honey

Saltbush is an arid species. A native Australian silver-sage-looking shrub, it grows tall, vast, and rampant in harsh climates, to which it is tolerant. As elucidated from the name, it is salty, yet also soft, earthy, and herbaceous, used not just for flavor but also its ability to heal. The plant is important to this land.

The leaves that I use are dried and ground, and I know it can't be sourced everywhere, but that's also what makes each bite of this cake precious. The same amount of summer savory, sage, or thyme can be used as a replacement.

/ *Serves 8* /

Adjust a rack to the middle of the oven, then preheat it to 350°F (180°C). Grease and line an 8-inch (20-cm) cake pan with parchment paper.

Line a baking sheet with parchment paper, then scatter the almonds over it. Roast for 8 to 10 minutes, until golden and fragrant. Cool, then blitz to a meal in a food processor. Tip into a medium bowl, then sift in the flour, baking powder, and salt. Whisk to combine.

In the bowl of a stand mixer that's fitted with the paddle attachment, cream the butter and sugar on medium speed until light and fluffy, 3 to 5 minutes. Pause to scrape, then beat in the honey and zest. Beat in the eggs, one at a time, incorporating well after each addition. Lower the speed, then tip in the dry ingredients and beat until just combined. Scrape the batter into the prepared pan, smoothing it out with an offset palette knife. Scatter with flaked almonds.

Bake for 50 minutes to an hour, until golden brown. You can tent the top with aluminum foil if it starts to darken toward the end. A skewer inserted into the middle should come out clean. Set onto a wire rack.

Next, make the syrup. Put the saltbush into a medium saucepan, then add the honey. Let it come to a foam over medium-high heat, then reduce the heat slightly. Simmer, swirling often, until the liquid has gone from gold to amber—it won't take longer than a few minutes. Pour it all over the cake. Let it soak and settle, then unmold.

Serve slightly warm or at room temperature. Leftovers can be sealed and stored in a cool, dark place for up to 3 days, during which time the flavor will intensify.

Salted Almond Granita

1½ cups (170 g) slivered almonds

Sicilian sea salt

1 cup (240 ml) almond milk

¼ cup (50 g) granulated sugar

1½ cups (360 ml) sparkling mineral water

Some wane, this granita swells. The salt hits in waves and envelops all with its icy, sluiced reach. I don't like to list a final measurement for it, as I've never wanted to be the arbiter of taste, only the guide, and most of the work to be done for this recipe is unseen—in idle hours, the hands-off time. We are forced to submit to its frozen rhythms, but make no mistake, there is a ferocity that lies inside.

/ ***Serves 4 to 6*** /

Put the almonds into a food processor and pulverize to form a smooth, thick, and creamy paste, stopping as needed to scrape the bowl. Season with salt, then blitz again. Transfer to a container, then re-measure it. You'll need ½ cup (130 g) of almond paste for this recipe.

Put the almond milk, sugar, and paste into a blender. Whir on low speed to combine. Taste and adjust again with salt, then pour the mixture into a large bowl. Stir in the sparkling water, then pour it all into a deep dish.

Freeze for a few hours, until just set. The time it takes will vary on your freezer and the dish used, so keep an eye on it. You want it to be semi-solid, not a mass. Stir and scrape with a fork to agitate until a fine, flaky, and shaved crystal-like texture has formed. Freeze again, leaving it alone for about an hour. Continue this process of stirring and refreezing a few more times, until voluminous and snowy.

Just before you're ready to serve, put your serving bowls into the freezer. Agitate the granita for a final time, then spoon it into the cold vessels. Eat immediately. It will keep, covered, in the coldest part of the freezer for about a week.

the sixth sense

A few shots of Amaretto to drown never goes astray.

Umami

How to put something into words that escapes ensnarement? ¶ Umami seems elusive, and that's partly due to the air of mystery that surrounds it. In the tale of taste, it wasn't universally accepted until much later, and thus comes with a wealth of mythology created to decipher it; to make it loved, feared, or understood. And like all myths that challenge us to reconcile our humanity, the fifth and final taste is big, strong, and a little disquieting, filled with enough electric charge to light up an ocean. I don't consider it visual, but aural, and it requires some handling to bring it into alignment with sweetness. ¶ A powerful flavoring agent useful to stir dessert, umami is often misunderstood, at times subjective but not without scientific foundation. At the heart of it is desire, a yen, for more, the word blurring the lines of "savory deliciousness" when translated from Japanese. The taste is rich, moreish, and palpable, with a constitution meant to coax the mouth into a fine fabric made of silk. I find myself at mercy when I eat it—primal and animalistic, but mostly nourished. ¶ It's all down to those amino acid glutamates, compounded in fermented, dried, or aged foods, processes that all take considerate tenderness, maturity, and time that are then reflected in a mouthful. Umami can easily become confused with the other four tastes, in particular salt, but the distinction becomes clear the more you encounter it, sometimes with softness, others pelt. In my head, I have it drawn as intricate and layered as Dante's Inferno, the nine circles a shade of umami, twisting deeper with each bite, or descent. ¶ These recipes show you the path—stick it straight or not, but the theme that courses through them all is that there is no final destination. They don't rush and emit the feeling that flavors, like roads, are meant to be traveled. "Let's take the long way home," I always say, which is how I find myself here, alive at the end of the earth, the closest to what I am—my sixth sense sated, at last.

Bubur Injin

FOR THE PUDDING

¾ cup (115 g) glutinous black rice

⅓ cup (50 g) glutinous white rice

2 pandan leaves

4 ounces (115 g) palm sugar, grated, plus more to serve

Flaky sea salt

FOR THE STICKY BANANAS

⅓ cup (75 g) unsalted butter, cubed

1 tablespoon white miso

½ cup (110 g) light brown sugar

A pinch of ground star anise

Zest from ½ a lime

2 large bananas

Coconut milk, to serve

I have this technique less down to science and more to instinct. Forbidden and fragrant, black rice pudding is something that I grew up eating, and while teachable, for me, its final resting place lies more in memory than anywhere else.

I first learned to make this recipe as a child, in Bali, sneaking into a cooking class my mother was taking. We were staying in a guesthouse of the school, so I could easily come and go as I pleased, and as it turns out, only when sweetness was being taught. I became immersed into a world that perfectly struck the balance between dark and light—as reflected in this dessert.

/ *Serves 4* /

START by soaking the black and white rice overnight, submerging the grains with enough water. The next morning, strain and rinse well. Transfer to a large stockpot. Fold and knot the pandan leaves and toss them in too, along with 4 cups (960 ml) water. Bring to a boil over medium-high heat, then lower to maintain a simmer, stirring frequently with a wooden spoon until creamy and porridge-like in consistency. It should take about half an hour, if not a little more. Discard the leaves and stir in the palm sugar and flaky salt until dissolved.

When the rice is almost done, make the sticky bananas. In a wide cast-iron skillet, combine the butter, miso, light brown sugar, star anise, and zest. Position over medium heat, whisking slowly, until the mixture is hot, bubbling, and melted. Meanwhile, slit the bananas lengthwise down the middle, skin and all. Position into the skillet, flesh side down. Cook, turning and basting as needed, until the fruit is caramelized, and the sauce is reduced. Discard the protective skins.

Ladle the pudding into bowls and serve, topped with the bananas, a swirl of coconut milk, and more palm sugar, if desired. This is best eaten warm, soon after making.

23. DEPOTISM.
THE JESUITS WERE EXPELLED FROM PORTUGAL AND FRANCE
DE LA COUR
DUKES OF SAVOY
EMPURER©
VITAPHONE
DANGER
HARDWARE
HUMAN CANNON BALL
GORILLA TELEPATHY
THE PEASANT
THE LAWYER
SOLAR ECLIPSE
CHAOS
BATTLE OF SAINTS
DEWEY DECIMAL SYSTEM
12. BARKING DOGS

Heaven and Hell Cake

FOR THE CAKE

2 cups + 2 tablespoons (265 g) all-purpose flour

1 cup (85 g) Carbon Black or Dutch processed cocoa powder

2 teaspoons baking soda

1 teaspoon baking powder

¾ teaspoon salt

1½ cups (300 g) granulated sugar

½ cup (110 g) light brown sugar

3 large eggs

½ cup + 1½ tablespoons (130 ml) vegetable oil

½ cup (120 g) sour cream

½ cup (120 ml) whole milk

1 cup + 2 tablespoons (270 ml) hot coffee

FOR THE SYRUP

½ cup + 1½ tablespoons (120 g) granulated sugar

FOR THE RED PEPPER REDUCTION

About 2 large (1 pound/450 g) red peppers

½ cup (100 g) granulated sugar

3 tablespoons honey

Juice from ½ a lemon

A pinch of salt

FOR THE BUTTERCREAM

½ cup (70 g) black sesame seeds

⅔ cup (115 g) chopped white chocolate

6 large egg whites

1¼ cups (250 g) granulated sugar

1¾ cups (400 g) unsalted butter, softened at room temperature

1 teaspoon vanilla extract

This is a cake held by the dark. Embattled, the initial flavors of sweetness and light soon dim, then disappear into the depths where they go on to thrive. I further the descent with a sticky-sweet reduction made of red peppers, which are singed until their cell walls disintegrate and blacken. The spice is subtle and constrained to the confines of each buttercream-filled layer, which is also where the predominant source of umami lies. Infernal but soothed, each bite is like taking the stairs straight down to the pit—or the core, hollow, crust—whatever place resides inside and that you wish to call it.

/ ***Serves 8 to 12*** /

Preheat the oven to 350°F (180°C). Grease and line three 7-inch (18-cm) cake pans with parchment paper.

Sift the flour, cocoa powder, baking soda, baking powder, and salt into a large bowl, then stir in the sugars. Make a well in the middle. In a separate bowl, whisk together the eggs, oil, sour cream, and milk. Pour into the dry ingredients and whisk in a clockwise motion until smooth, thick, and muddied. Whisk in the coffee. Divide the batter among the prepared pans.

Bake for 30 to 35 minutes, until springy to the touch. A skewer inserted into the middle of the cakes should come out clean. Leave to cool in the pans for 15 minutes, then turn out and onto a wire rack to cool completely.

Meanwhile, make the syrup. Put the sugar and ½ cup (120 ml) water into a small saucepan. Bring to a boil over medium heat, stirring often to dissolve the granules, then remove and cool. Level off the domed cake tops and brush them with syrup.

Next, make the reduction. Scorch the red peppers over an open flame or under a broiler until the skin is blistered, burnt, and weeping. De-core and de-seed. Transfer to a blender and pulverize to a purée. Pass through a fine-mesh sieve into a medium saucepan, easing it through with the assistance of a rubber spatula, then add the sugar, honey, and lemon juice. Stir over medium-low heat until compote-like, about 7 to 10 minutes. It should cling and hold to the back of the spoon before softly falling away when it's done. Add the salt, then transfer into a medium heatproof bowl and cool to room temperature before use. You won't need all of it—but it's easier to make in a large batch than small.

(cont.)

Start the buttercream by toasting the black sesame seeds in a dry skillet until crackling. Cool, then grind to a gritty paste in a food processor or spice grinder. You won't need to take it as far as tahini—textural is fine.

Place the white chocolate into a medium heatproof bowl. Set it over a saucepan that's filled with a few inches of barely simmering water. Do not let the base of the bowl touch the water below. Stir over medium-low heat until melted. Remove and set aside.

Next, put the egg whites and sugar into the bowl of a stand mixer and set it over the same saucepan that's still filled with a few inches of barely simmering water. Heat, whisking often, until it reaches 160°F (71°C) on a thermometer. The sugar granules will have dissolved and the mixture will be sticky-hot to the touch. Transfer to the mixer and fit with the whisk attachment. Whisk on medium-high speed until a thick and glossy meringue has formed, about 7 minutes. Switch out the whisk for the paddle attachment, then lower the speed to medium. Beat in the butter, a tablespoon at a time, until all incorporated. Beat in the white chocolate, followed by the black sesame paste, and vanilla. Continue to beat to form a silky buttercream.

To assemble, set a cake layer onto a serving plate, cut side facing up. Spread over a few tablespoons of the buttercream, smoothing it almost to the edges with an offset palette knife. Slick the buttercream to form a dam around the rim, then spoon in droplets of the red pepper reduction, the amount used to your personal heat preference. Press on the next layer, cut side facing down. Again, frost with buttercream and fill with reduction. Add on the final layer. Coat the cake in thick swoops and swirls with the last of the buttercream. Transfer to the refrigerator and chill until just set, before serving. This is best eaten on the day of making, and once cut should be loosely covered and kept in the refrigerator, where it'll last for 3 to 5 days. Allow time for slices to return to room temperature before serving.

Black Sesame Croustillant Cookies

FOR THE COOKIES

1½ cups + 1 teaspoon (190 g) all-purpose flour

¾ cup (65 g) Dutch processed cocoa powder, plus more for dusting

¼ teaspoon salt

¾ cup + 1 teaspoon (175 g) unsalted butter, softened at room temperature

¾ cup (150 g) granulated sugar

1 large egg

FOR THE CROUSTILLANT

1 cup + 2 tablespoons (160 g) cashews

½ cup (70 g) black sesame seeds

⅔ cup (135 g) granulated sugar

½ teaspoon smoked salt

FOR THE GANACHE

1 cup (170 g) finely chopped dark chocolate

⅔ cup (160 ml) heavy cream

1 tablespoon black sesame oil

FOR THE BUTTERCREAM

⅔ cup (150 g) unsalted butter, softened at room temperature

2½ cups (300 g) confectioners' sugar, sifted

3 tablespoons heavy cream

1 teaspoon vanilla extract

I like the selfishness of these. Cookies, naturally, are an indulgent act, but add a second layer, along with a thick middle of buttercream and ganache, as well as a caramelized coating, and it's even more so. The trick is to resist the rich overwhelm, while still wanting more. I do it with black sesame seeds. They're the dark tetrad types of the pastry world. Covert, intense, and addictive—they take out the sweet and answer to no one.

/ *Makes 21 cookies* /

For the cookies, whisk together the flour, cocoa powder, and salt in a medium mixing bowl.

In the bowl of a stand mixer that's fitted with the paddle attachment, beat the butter and sugar on medium speed until pale and creamy, 3 to 5 minutes. Pause to scrape down the bowl, then beat in the egg. Lower the speed and beat in the dry ingredients until combined. Scrape the sticky dough onto a sheet of plastic wrap and divide it in half. Cover and chill for at least an hour.

Adjust racks to the top, middle, and bottom thirds of the oven, then preheat it to 325°F (160°C). Line three baking sheets with parchment paper.

Unwrap the dough onto a surface that's dusted lightly with cocoa. Roll it out until it's about ¼ inch (.6 cm) thick, then with a 2.3-inch (6-cm) circular cutter, stamp out as many rounds from it as possible. Lift off with an offset palette knife and divide them among the prepared sheets, leaving some space apart for spreading. Reroll the scraps and repeat with the remaining dough. Dust as needed to prevent sticking.

Bake for 8 minutes, rotating halfway through, or until dry. Cool on the sheets for a few minutes, then transfer onto a wire rack to cool completely. Meanwhile, make the croustillant.

Raise the oven heat to 350°F (180°C). Scatter the cashews and black sesame seeds into an even layer on a lined baking sheet. Roast for 10 minutes, or until fragrant.

Next, put the sugar into a medium saucepan, along with ¼ cup (60 ml) water. Bring to a boil, stirring often to dissolve the granules, then raise the heat to high. Continue to cook until it reaches 250°F (121°C) on a candy

(*cont.*)

thermometer. Remove and tip in the cashews, seeds, and the salt. Stir vigorously with a wooden spoon until a fine coating of crystallized white sugar has formed. Transfer the mixture into a separate clean saucepan. Again, set it over high heat. Continue to cook until the sugar has started to taint, and then gradually reduce the heat so that it can cook down for as low, slow, and long as possible. Push the nuts and seeds around occasionally for even coloring. Tip back onto the baking sheet and leave to harden. Grind roughly with a mortar and pestle.

To make the ganache, put the chocolate into a medium heatproof bowl and pour the cream into a saucepan. Bring it to a simmer over gentle heat, then stream over the chocolate. Stand for a minute, then stir until smooth. Stir in the oil. Cool on the kitchen counter until spreadable.

For the buttercream, in the bowl of a stand mixer that's fitted with the whisk attachment, beat the butter, confectioners' sugar, cream, and vanilla on medium speed until fluffy. Scrape it into a piping bag that's fitted with a ½-inch (1.3-cm) round tip.

When you're ready to assemble, transfer the croustillant to a rimmed dish. Turn over half the cookies, pipe on a ring of buttercream to create an outer border, fill it with ganache, and sandwich with a mate. Roll in croustillant—so that it sticks.

These will keep, stored in an airtight container, in a cool, dark place for 2 to 3 days.

Comté Custard Choux

Comté is a cheese that speaks deeply of its surroundings. I find that it encompasses almost all of taste: sweet, sour, salt, and sometimes a little bitterness, with a tertiary tilt toward umami as it matures. Its dulcet nature is at home in this custard, the crackled choux, enveloping.

/ ***Makes 32 buns*** /

FOR THE CUSTARD

2½ cups (600 ml) whole milk

1 vanilla bean

⅔ cup (135 g) granulated sugar

6 large egg yolks

¼ cup + 1 teaspoon (35 g) cornstarch

3 tablespoons unsalted butter, at room temperature

½ cup (40 g) finely grated Comté cheese

FOR THE CRAQUELIN

½ cup (1 stick/115 g) unsalted butter, softened at room temperature

½ cup + 1 teaspoon (115 g) light brown sugar

¾ cup + 2½ tablespoons (115 g) all-purpose flour

FOR THE CHOUX

½ cup (120 ml) whole milk

1 teaspoon granulated sugar

¼ teaspoon salt

½ cup (1 stick/115 g) unsalted butter, cubed

1 cup + 2 tablespoons (140 g) all-purpose flour

4 large eggs

Confectioners' sugar, to finish

To make the custard, pour the milk into a large saucepan, then slit open the vanilla bean and scrape out the seeds. Add them into the pan, along with the pod too. Bring to a simmer over gentle heat. Meanwhile, in a medium heatproof bowl, whisk together the sugar, egg yolks, and cornstarch. As soon as the liquid has reached temperature, stream a little of it into the yolks, whisking to combine, and discarding the pod. Transfer the mixture back into the pan. Continue to heat, whisking slowly and constantly, until smooth, thick, and glossy. Whisk in the butter and Comté. Scrape the custard into a large heatproof bowl, then cover the surface with plastic wrap. Chill until completely cold.

Next, make the craquelin. In the bowl of a stand mixer that's fitted with the paddle attachment, beat the butter and light brown sugar until creamy and light caramel in color, about 3 minutes. Pause to scrape down the bowl, then tip in the flour. Beat on low speed to form damp clumps. Scrape, gather, and bring it together into a smooth ball.

Between two sheets of parchment paper, roll the dough out until it's about ⅛ inch (.3 cm) thick, repositioning the paper as needed to avoid tearing or creasing. Set onto a baking sheet and freeze until firm enough to handle, then, with a 1¾-inch (4.5-cm) circular cutter, stamp out as many rounds from it as possible. Lift off with an offset palette knife, and transfer them to a separate lined baking sheet. Reroll the scraps and repeat. Freeze until needed.

Adjust racks to the top, middle, and bottom thirds of the oven, then preheat it to 375°F (190°C). Line three baking sheets with parchment paper.

For the choux, combine the milk, sugar, and salt in a wide saucepan. Pour in ½ cup (120 ml) water and add the butter. With a wooden spoon, stir over medium heat until melted. Bring to a boil, then slide the pan off the heat and tip in the flour. Work vigorously to incorporate and smooth out any lumps. Return to the heat and keep stirring for a few more minutes,

(cont.)

until the dough balls together. A thin film will have lined the base of the pan. Transfer into a stand mixer, then fit with the paddle attachment. Beat on high speed until the steam has escaped and the bowl is no longer hot to the touch. Beat in the eggs, one at a time, and waiting until fully incorporated before adding in the next. The mixture will split at first, then quickly pull together and blend into a velvetlike paste. Scrape into a pastry bag that's fitted with a ½-inch (1.3-cm) round tip.

Holding the bag at a slight angle, pipe out 1¾-inch (4.5-cm) sized rounds onto the prepared sheets, leaving space apart for spreading. You should aim to fit 9 to 12 choux per sheet. Top each with a craquelin cutout, pressing lightly to adhere.

Bake for 25 minutes, then rotate and bake for another 10 minutes—resisting the temptation to open the oven door, or risk deflation. The puffs will be deeply golden and feel hollow to the touch upon exit. Turn off the oven and remove the puffs. Prick the tip of a sharp knife into the bases of each, rotating it around to create a hole that's just wide enough to pipe through. Return to the oven and prop open the door. Cool in the residual heat.

To fill, scrape the custard into a piping bag that's fitted with a ½-inch (1.3-cm) round tip. Bloat the choux through their bases, being careful not to overflow. Wipe away any excess, then dust the tops with confectioners' sugar. Serve soon after.

These are best eaten on the day of making, or close to it, as they'll soften with time. Store leftovers in an airtight container in the refrigerator for up to 3 days.

the sixth sense

If time is of the essence, craquelin is not. It's a finicky component that can be made in advance and kept in the freezer, but sometimes I like to alter this recipe into something else entirely. A flourish of pearl sugar instead of the craquelin top turns these pastry puffs into a gougère-chouquette Frankenstein hybrid that's equally interesting, without the pressure.

Wakame and White Chocolate Ice Cream

1¼ cups (300 ml) whole milk, plus more for replenishing

1 tablespoon (3 g) dried wakame flakes

1⅔ cups + 2 tablespoons (430 ml) heavy cream

5 large egg yolks

½ cup + 1 tablespoon (115 g) granulated sugar

1 teaspoon vanilla extract

1 cup (170 g) finely chopped white chocolate

Wakame was introduced to Australian waters on the hulls of visiting ships. An invasive species, it has to be harvested and harnessed or it threatens to engulf. Its encroaching nature is also evident in how it tastes. Wild and brackish, wakame is on the saltier side of umami, but with a mild, satiny sweetness. There's no need to go overboard with it, though; dried, its flavor is concentrated, and I use it to form the base of this enriched ice cream. An antithesis, the white chocolate is softer and silkier, infused with seaweed.

/ *Serves 4* /

Put the milk and wakame into a medium saucepan. Bring to a simmer over a gentle heat, then turn off and leave to infuse for half an hour.

Strain the milk from the swollen seaweed into a large heavy-bottomed saucepan, pressing on the backs to release any infused juices. Re-measure the milk. You'll have lost a little during the steep, so replenish it to the total amount called for. Pour in the cream, then bring to a simmer over medium heat.

Meanwhile, in a medium heatproof bowl, whisk together the egg yolks, sugar, and vanilla. Place the white chocolate into a separate heatproof bowl.

Slip a ladle of the hot liquid into the yolks, whisking as it's added to acclimatize, then ladle in another and whisk until combined. Transfer it all back into the pan on the stove. Continue to gently heat, stirring until the mixture is thick enough to coat the back of a spoon, 5 to 6 minutes. If you have a thermometer, it should fall within a range of 170°F to 180°F (77°C to 82°C). Stream it all over the chocolate and stir until melted. Cover with plastic wrap and chill for at least 8 hours, but preferably overnight.

When you're ready to churn, place a container or aluminum loaf pan into the freezer to keep cold. Pour the chilled base into an ice cream machine. Churn according to the manufacturer's instructions. It should be soft serve–like when done. Extract into the par-frozen container, then cover with aluminum foil and freeze until just firm before serving. It will keep, covered, in the coldest part of the freezer for a week.

Soy Ganache Brownies

Often, I lose myself in darkness. I believe it was Dostoyevsky who said the darker the night, the brighter the stars, with a reference to grief and God, but I don't dare touch that. Soy ganache may sound strange, and if I confess, it kind of is, but it has a salinity that gives these rich brownies a line of clarity for the mouth to follow—a path out of the dark, if you will.

/ *Makes 20 brownies* /

FOR THE BROWNIES

1 cup + 2 tablespoons (140 g) all-purpose flour

¾ cup + 2 tablespoons (75 g) Dutch processed cocoa powder

¾ teaspoon baking powder

½ teaspoon salt

1⅓ cups (230 g) finely chopped dark chocolate

1 cup (2 sticks/230 g) unsalted butter, cubed

4 large eggs

2 cups (440 g) dark brown sugar

FOR THE GANACHE

⅔ cup (160 ml) heavy cream

2 tablespoons soy sauce

1 cup (170 g) finely chopped dark chocolate

Adjust a rack to the middle of the oven, then preheat it to 350°F (180°C). Grease and line an 8-inch (20-cm) square pan with parchment paper, leaving a slight sling over the sides.

Whisk together the flour, cocoa powder, baking powder, and salt in a medium mixing bowl.

Put the chocolate into a medium heatproof bowl and set it near to the space where you'll be working. Add the butter to a saucepan and heat over medium-high heat, stirring often, until melted. Raise the heat and continue to cook, swirling often but without stirring, until a nutty brown liquid has formed. It will foam, hiss, and crackle, but subside as it nears done. Add in with the chocolate, scraping in any burnt bits, and stir until melted.

Next, in the bowl of a stand mixer that's fitted with the whisk attachment, whisk the eggs and dark brown sugar on medium-high speed until thick and voluminous, about 3 minutes. Lower the speed and stream in the melted chocolate mixture. Whisk in the dry ingredients until glossy and uniform. Scrape into the prepared pan, smoothing out to the edges.

Bake for 35 to 40 minutes, until shiny, crackled, and just set. The middle should still retain a squidge. Transfer to a wire rack and leave to cool in the pan completely.

To make the ganache, bring the cream and soy to a simmer in a small saucepan over medium heat. Meanwhile, put the chocolate into a medium heatproof bowl. When the liquid has reached temperature, pour it all over the chocolate. Stand for a minute, then stir until smooth. Leave to cool and thicken on the kitchen counter until spreadable. Smooth all over the brownie and let it set.

Carefully lift the slab out from the pan, and then with a sharp knife, slice it into even squares. They're intense—I cut about 20. These are best eaten on the day of making and will keep, stored in an airtight container, in the refrigerator for up to 3 days.

the sixth sense

Gild the lily with smoked salt.

Yeasted Chocolate Chunk Cookies

3 cups (375 g) all-purpose flour

1¼ teaspoons instant dried yeast

1 teaspoon baking soda

½ teaspoon salt

2 cups (2 sticks/230 g) unsalted butter, softened at room temperature

1 cup (220 g) light brown sugar

⅔ cup (135 g) granulated sugar

1 large egg

1 tablespoon vanilla extract

1½ cups (255 g) chopped dark chocolate

Flaky sea salt, for finishing

The taste of yeast is pervasive. It devours, literally, needing sustenance, sweetness, and warmth to survive. Even if you have nothing to give it, it will find something to feed on, and because of its hunger, it's able to elicit that infamous umami taste.

These cookies aren't the thin and crisp kind. They're soft and chewy, the yeast operating as a flavoring agent as well as leavening. I feed the dough only a tiny bit, but if there's anything I know for sure, it's that even the smallest act can alter the end.

/ *Makes 24 cookies* /

Adjust racks to the top, middle, and bottom thirds of the oven, then preheat it to 350°F (180°C). Line three baking sheets with parchment paper.

Whisk together the flour, yeast, baking soda, and salt in a medium mixing bowl.

In the bowl of a stand mixer that's fitted with the paddle attachment, or using handheld electric beaters, beat the butter and sugars on medium speed until pale and creamy, about 3 minutes. Pause to scrape down the bowl, then resume, and beat in the egg and vanilla. Lower the speed, then beat in the dry ingredients until just combined. Beat in the chocolate chunks until evenly distributed.

Using a medium 2¾-inch (7-cm) scoop, or generous tablespoon as a measure, portion out the dough into mounds, rolling each into smooth balls in the palm of your hand. Divide among the prepared sheets, leaving a few inches of space apart for spreading. Flourish with flaky salt.

Bake for 12 to 14 minutes, rotating halfway through, until light golden. The edges should be crisp and the centers slightly soft. Cool for a few minutes, then lift the cookies off the sheets onto a wire rack to cool further before serving. They'll keep well, stored in an airtight container at room temperature, for about 3 days.

Vegemite Flowing Heart Cake

FOR THE HEART

½ cup (120 ml) heavy cream

½ cup (85 g) chopped dark chocolate

1 teaspoon Vegemite

FOR THE CAKES

⅔ cup (115 g) chopped dark chocolate

⅓ cup (75 g) unsalted butter, cubed

2 large eggs

⅓ cup (70 g) granulated sugar

⅓ cup (42 g) all-purpose flour

2 tablespoons Dutch processed cocoa powder, plus more for dusting

Crème fraîche, for serving

It was acclaimed French chef Michel Bras who posited that all versions of coulants au chocolat are the result of an idea, an emotion. This recipe is founded in memory. The cake is intensely dark, as is the heart, comprised of a fluid ganache condensed with Vegemite. Only a teaspoon of the contentious paste is used, but that's enough for its presence to be felt. I call it an "Australian umami." Salty, yeasted, and tar-like, it can be disquieting to a virgin palate—but nonetheless pleasurable.

/ *Serves 4* /

First, prepare the heart. Put the cream, chocolate, and Vegemite into a medium heatproof bowl, then set it over a saucepan that's filled with a few inches of barely simmering water. Do not let the base of the bowl touch the water below. Stir over gentle heat until melted, then remove. Chill the ganache until it is solid enough to scoop—about an hour.

Adjust a rack to the middle of the oven, then preheat it to 350°F (180°C). Generously butter four 2½ x 2½-inch/5-ounce (6.5 x 6.5-cm/150-ml) dariole molds. Dust the insides with cocoa powder, then tap out the excess. Place them onto a baking sheet.

For the cakes, melt down the chocolate and butter in a double boiler. Set aside.

Next, in the bowl of a stand mixer that's fitted with the whisk attachment, whisk the eggs and sugar on medium-high speed until pale, thick, and voluminous, about 3 to 5 minutes. It should softly fall back onto itself in a flowing trail when the whisk is lifted. Sift over the flour and cocoa, then, with a rubber spatula, fold until almost combined. Drizzle over the melted chocolate mixture and gently fold it in. Divide among the prepared molds, filling a third of the way full, then form an indent in the middle of each. Fill it with 2 teaspoons of the heart—do not let the ganache touch the sides of the ramekin. Cover with the remaining batter.

Bake for 13 to 14 minutes, until risen and springy to the touch. Rest for a minute, then invert carefully onto plates. Eat immediately, with crème fraîche on top to cut through the darkness.

Roasted Quince and Reserved Rind Cream

FOR THE CREAM

5 cups (1200 ml) heavy cream

Rind cut from a wheel of Parmigiano-Reggiano (about 2¾ ounces/80 g)

2 tablespoons + 1 teaspoon light brown sugar

1 teaspoon vanilla extract

FOR THE QUINCE

4 cups (800 g) granulated sugar

1¼ cups (300 ml) sherry

Juice from 1 lemon and a thick strip of peel

2 star anise

1 bay leaf

2 large (about 2¼ pounds/1 kg) quince

I think that slow-roasting quince is the only way to cook them. Their bodies blush with exposure to time, sugar, and heat, and require little alongside to make them sing. Early in my cooking, I started to reserve parmesan rinds for the bases of broths and stocks, which slowly became creams and custards. My favorite way to use them is also performed in the oven, and from my heritage.

In Russian, we called it *ryazhenka,* where dairy is baked for an enduringly long amount of time until a protective crust is formed—a delicacy. I make this one with cream and throw in the often-discarded rinds, as well as some sugar, which results in a caramelized liquid full of flavor. Whip it softly and serve it with the blushing fruit.

/ *Serves 4 to 6* /

Adjust a rack to the middle of the oven, then preheat it to 225°F (110°C).

In a large dutch oven or ceramic roasting dish, combine the cream, rind, and 1 teaspoon of the light brown sugar. Bake undisturbed until a golden, thin, and shattering crust has formed on the surface, about 1½ to 2 hours, depending on your dish. Remove and cool, then skim the top and remove the rind. Strain the liquid into a large bowl and chill thoroughly.

Adjust the oven heat to 275°F (130°C).

For the quince, put the sugar, sherry, lemon juice and peel, star anise, and bay into a stockpot. Stir in 3 cups (720 ml) water. Bring to a simmer over medium heat. Meanwhile, peel the quince and cut them into quarters, forcing out the seeds and cores. Place into the pot. Bring to a boil, then remove from the heat. Tip it all into a 4-cup (1-L) capacity roasting dish, sheathing the top with parchment paper and slitting out a vent. Tent with aluminum foil. Bake for about 3 hours, then unveil and cook for another hour or so. The quince should be crimson and tender. Leave to cool in the syrup.

When you're ready to serve, strain the infused cream into the bowl of a stand mixer that's fitted with the whisk attachment. Add the remaining 2 tablespoons of light brown sugar, along with the vanilla. Whisk on medium speed to supportive peaks.

Serve the quince with the cream and residual syrup. Leftovers can be covered and stored in the refrigerator to be eaten within 3 to 5 days.

Crunchy Chili Oil Tart

FOR THE CRUST

1½ cups + 1 teaspoon (190 g) all-purpose flour

⅓ cup + 1 tablespoon (30 g) Dutch processed cocoa powder

¼ cup (30 g) confectioners' sugar

¼ teaspoon salt

⅔ cup (150 g) unsalted butter, cold and cut into ½-inch (1.3-cm) cubes

2 large egg yolks

1 large egg white, whisked with 1 teaspoon water, for the wash

FOR THE FILLING

¾ cup + 1 tablespoon (115 g) unsalted peanuts

¾ cup (150 g) granulated sugar

A pinch of salt

1½ cups (255 g) finely chopped 55 to 60% dark chocolate

1¼ cups (300 ml) heavy cream

FOR THE GANACHE

¾ cup (130 g) finely chopped 70% dark chocolate

¾ cup + 2 tablespoons (210 ml) heavy cream

2 tablespoons unsalted butter, softened at room temperature

Crunchy chili oil

I was raised with a desire to fear MSG. My mother held that infamous red book of chemicals close to the chest and would siren off the alarm, "621—AVOID MSG IN ALL ITS DISGUISES." But I don't really care about a bad reputation, for where MSG frightens, umami thrills.

Crunchy chili oil has a reputation of its own. My dear friend Sarah, of Ugly Food and Co, makes the best. It almost glows hot like danger, and goes head-to-head with the fabled jars of Lao Gan Ma, or Old Godmother. I need heat to balance this tart, and the oil doesn't distract, but instead lifts. Spoon it over scant or sparingly, but challenge your trepidation.

/ *Serves 8* /

To make the crust, whisk together the flour, cocoa powder, confectioners' sugar, and salt in a large mixing bowl. Add the butter and toss to coat. Begin to rub and blend the cubes into the dry ingredients, until mostly pea-sized pieces remain. Add the yolks and mix with a wooden spoon to combine. Bring the dough together into a ball, then shape it into a disc. Cover with plastic wrap and chill for at least an hour.

Position a 10-inch (25-cm) tart tin with a removable base onto a baking sheet. Flour a work surface, then unwrap the chilled dough onto it and dust the top lightly too. With a wooden pin, roll it into a circle that's about ⅛ inch (.3 cm) thick and a few inches larger than the tin you're using. Carefully lift and fit, then trim off the excess overhang. Transfer to the freezer while you adjust a rack to the middle of the oven and preheat it to 350°F (180°C).

Line the crust with a sheet of parchment paper, then fill it to the brim with ceramic weights or dried beans. Bake for 20 minutes. Remove and leave to cool slightly, then discard the weights. Coat lightly with egg wash. Return to the oven and continue to bake for another 10 minutes, or until set. Transfer to a wire rack and cool completely.

To make the filling, scatter the peanuts into an even layer across a lined baking sheet. Stir the sugar and ¼ cup (60 ml) water together in a small saucepan. Bring to a boil over medium heat, then raise the heat to high and continue to cook until deep amber in color. Immediately pour it all over the nuts, then add the salt. Leave to harden, then break into shards. Blitz into dust in a food processor.

Next, put the chocolate into a medium heatproof bowl. Pour the cream into a saucepan and bring it to a simmer. Stream all over the chocolate, then stir until smooth. Stir in two-thirds of the praline dust. Smooth over the crust, then refrigerate until set, about an hour.

To finish, make the ganache. Again, place the chocolate into a medium heatproof bowl and add the cream into a saucepan. Bring to a simmer, then pour it all over the chocolate and stir until smooth. Add the butter and stir until dissolved. Smooth the ganache over the tart. Chill again, but this time until just set—less than an hour.

Remove the tart from the tin and slide it onto a plate. Spoon over enough crunchy chili oil and then scatter with the remaining praline. Slice into wedges with a warm, sharp knife and then serve. It'll keep, loosely covered, in the refrigerator, for 2 to 3 days.

Speck Sticky Buns

FOR THE DOUGH

4 cups (500 g) all-purpose flour

⅓ cup (70 g) granulated sugar

2½ teaspoons (10 g) instant dried yeast

½ teaspoon finely chopped rosemary

1 teaspoon salt

4 large eggs

⅔ cup (150 ml) whole milk

¾ cup + 2 tablespoons (200 g) unsalted butter, softened at room temperature

FOR THE TOPPING

1¼ cups (180 g) pecans

Extra-virgin olive oil

½ cup (65 g) diced speck with rind removed (¼-inch/.6-cm pieces)

⅓ cup + 1 tablespoon (90 g) unsalted butter, cubed

¾ cup + 1 teaspoon (170 g) light brown sugar

¾ cup + 1 tablespoon (195 ml) heavy cream

¼ cup (85 ml) maple syrup

FOR THE FILLING

½ cup (110 g) light brown sugar

2 tablespoons granulated sugar

2 teaspoons ground cinnamon

¼ cup (60 g) unsalted butter, melted

My list of vices is long, but this recipe erases a fair few. The traits of speck are thick and fat, which also is a perfect description for the buns. Salty, sweet, and smoky, the cured meat goes head-to-head with all. They're meant for immediate consumption, best eaten warm and pliant, the caramel seeping.

/ *Makes 9 to 12 buns* /

To make the dough, put the flour, sugar, yeast, rosemary, and salt into the bowl of a stand mixer that's fitted with the dough hook attachment. Mix on low speed to combine, then add the eggs and milk. Knead on medium speed for a few minutes until rough and shaggy. Raise the speed. Continue to knead for a few more minutes, until the dough has begun to catch and then pull away from the sides of the bowl. Add a tablespoon of butter at a time, waiting until blended before adding the next. Knead until silky and elastic, 6 to 8 more minutes. Transfer to a greased large bowl. Cover with plastic wrap and leave to rise in a warm place until doubled in size, about 2 hours.

Preheat the oven to 350°F (180°C). Line a baking sheet with parchment paper and scatter over the pecans. Roast until golden and fragrant, 8 to 10 minutes. Cool, then chop.

Slip a little oil into a skillet to coat. Add the speck and fry over medium heat for a few minutes, until golden. Transfer to a small bowl and set aside. Put the butter into the pan, then lower the heat. Let it melt, then add the light brown sugar, cream, and maple syrup. Bring to a simmer, then reduce the heat and cook until the sauce is glossy and thick, about 3 to 5 minutes. Remove and stir in the pecans and speck. Transfer into the base of a deep 9 x 13-inch (23 x 33-cm) baking dish.

Next, for the filling, stir together the sugars and cinnamon in a small mixing bowl. Turn the dough out onto a floured work surface and lightly dust the top. With a wooden pin, roll it into a rough rectangle that's about ½ inch (1.3 cm) thick. Brush it with butter, then scatter on the spiced sugar mixture. Starting with the longest edge, roll into a taut log-shaped cylinder. Pinch the ends to seal, then flip it, so that the seam is facing down. With a sharp serrated knife or a looped piece of kitchen twine, slice 1½-inch (3.8-cm) thick pieces. Nestle them into the dish. Cover and leave to rise until just under doubled in size, about half an hour.

Meanwhile, adjust a rack to the middle of the oven, then preheat it to 350°F (180°C).

Bake for 40 to 45 minutes, until golden brown and bubbling. Stand for a few minutes, then carefully invert the buns out and onto a shallow plate. Spoon over any sticky remnants, and serve soon after, warm. These are best eaten on the day of making.

Deep Miso Caramel Apple Pie

FOR THE PASTRY

⅔ cup (150) unsalted butter, softened at room temperature

⅓ cup (70 g) granulated sugar

1 large egg

1 large egg yolk

2¼ cups (280 g) all-purpose flour

1 teaspoon baking powder

FOR THE CARAMEL

1 cup (200 g) granulated sugar

½ cup (120 ml) heavy cream

¼ cup (60 g) unsalted butter, cubed

2 tablespoons red miso

FOR THE FILLING

2½ pounds (1.1 kg) apples, like Golden Delicious, Pink Lady, Granny Smith, or Honeycrisp, or a combination

Juice from 1 lemon

1 tablespoon granulated sugar

¼ teaspoon ground cinnamon

¼ teaspoon ground cloves

¼ teaspoon ground ginger

Seeds scraped from 1 vanilla bean

Heavy cream, for brushing

Raw sugar, to coat

I like a warped, hapless pie. One with lumps, bumps, and divots that's tender, encasing, and soft—so soft, in fact, that you can spot the silhouette of fruit beneath. The pastry here isn't the usual kind, but it does disintegrate, operating more as a cloak than a blanket. But the best part is the caramel; made with red miso, it has an unmistakable concentration.

/ *Serves 6* /

To make the pastry, put the butter and sugar into the bowl of a stand mixer that's fitted with the paddle attachment. Beat on medium speed until pale and creamy, 3 to 4 minutes. Pause to scrape down the bowl, then beat in the egg and yolk. Lower the speed. Mix in the flour and baking powder until just combined. Some dry pockets should remain. With your hands, gather the dough up into a ball, then divide it and softly flatten each half into a disc. Cover with plastic wrap and chill for at least an hour or up to a day.

To make the caramel, scatter half of the sugar across the base of a wide saucepan, then set it over medium-high heat. Cook, agitating occasionally, until tinged golden. Scatter in the rest of the sugar, shaking to incorporate. Continue to cook until an amber-hued liquid has formed. Slide off from the heat and stream in the cream. It'll sputter, so add with caution. Whisk in the butter and miso. Pour into a medium heatproof bowl and cool before use.

Adjust a rack to the middle of the oven, then preheat it to 400°F (200°C). Place a 9-inch (23-cm) pie dish onto a rimmed baking sheet.

Peel and core the apples, chopping them into ¾-inch (2-cm) thick wedges. Toss into a large mixing bowl, along with the lemon juice, sugar, cinnamon, cloves, ginger, and vanilla seeds.

Unwrap the pastry onto a floured work surface, and lightly dust the top. With a wooden pin, roll it into a circle that's about ¼ inch (.6 cm) thick. It's a soft dough, and likes to stick, so readjust and flour as necessary. Fit it into the dish. Tip in the apples, then pour over the caramel.

Unwrap the remaining pastry and roll it out in the same manner as above. Transfer over the top, lidding, to form a pie. Trim off the excess pastry to an inch beyond the rim, then flute or crimp to seal. Brush with cream and sprinkle with a pinch of raw sugar. Slit a vent.

Bake for 45 minutes to an hour, until golden and bubbling. Stand until just warm, before serving the pie with cream or ice cream, for a temperamental collision. This is best eaten on the day of making. Keep leftovers covered in the refrigerator for 2 to 3 days.

Hojicha Marjolaine

This is an elaborate cake, a "doyenne," if you will, with a pedigree that goes back to revered French chef Fernand Point. It's meant to be stacked sky-high with layers of nutty meringue and enriched with two sorts of buttercream as well as ganache. I don't depart from his lead, but do add hojicha, an umami-laden roasted green tea, to heighten. The kind I use is full of earth, toast, and smoke, finely ground, and dark.

/ *Serves 8 to 10* /

FOR THE DACQUOISE

⅔ cup (75 g) almonds

⅔ cup (75 g) hazelnuts

1 teaspoon hojicha powder

6 large egg whites

¼ teaspoon cream of tartar

1 cup (200 g) granulated sugar

FOR THE PRALINE

⅔ cup (75 g) almonds

¾ cup (150 g) granulated sugar

A pinch of salt

FOR THE GANACHE

1⅔ cups (280 g) finely chopped dark chocolate

1½ cups (360 ml) heavy cream

FOR THE BUTTERCREAM

1 cup (200 g) granulated sugar

6 large egg yolks

1½ cups + 1 teaspoon (350 g) unsalted butter, softened at room temperature

2 teaspoons vanilla bean paste

2 tablespoons Cognac, optional, for assembly

Adjust a rack to the middle of the oven, then preheat it to 350°F (180°C). Grease and line a 12½ x 9-inch (32 x 23-cm) rimmed quarter sheet pan with parchment paper. Scatter over the almonds and hazelnuts. Roast for 10 minutes, or until golden brown. Cool, then tip into a food processor, along with the hojicha. Blitz to a coarse meal and set aside.

Lower the oven heat to 300°F (150°C).

In the bowl of a stand mixer that's fitted with the whisk attachment, whisk the egg whites and cream of tartar on medium speed to soft peaks. Add the sugar, a tablespoon at a time, until it's all used up. Continue to whisk until thick and glossy, then fold in the nut mixture. Scrape into the prepared pan, spreading it out with an offset palette knife.

Bake for 45 to 50 minutes, until light golden and crisp to the touch. Turn off the heat and pry open the oven door. Leave the dacquoise to cool inside until it reaches room temperature.

Next, make the praline. Scatter the almonds onto a lined baking sheet. Put the sugar into a medium saucepan, along with 3 tablespoons water. Bring to a boil over high heat, swirling as it begins to caramelize. Cook until deep amber in color. Remove, then immediately pour it all over the almonds. Add the salt and stand until hardened. Coarsely crush the praline and then place the pieces into a food processor. Pulverize into dust.

When you're ready to assemble, make the ganache. Put the chocolate into a medium heatproof bowl and pour the cream into a saucepan. Bring the cream to a simmer over gentle heat, then stream it all over the chocolate. Stir until smooth. Cool on the kitchen counter until spreadable—usually the time it takes to complete the next steps.

For the buttercream, put the sugar into a medium saucepan, along with ¼ cup (60 ml) water. Cook over medium-high heat until it reaches 250°F (121°C) on a candy thermometer. Meanwhile, start whisking the egg yolks in the bowl of a stand mixer fitted with the whisk attachment on medium speed. As soon as the syrup has come to temperature, stream it into the whisking yolks. Raise the speed and continue to whisk until thick and glossy. All the steam will have escaped and the bowl will no longer be hot to the touch. Switch out the whisk for the paddle attachment. Beat in the butter, a tablespoon at a time, followed by the vanilla bean paste. Continue to beat to form a silky buttercream. Scrape half of it into a medium bowl and set aside for assembly. Add half of the praline into the remaining buttercream and beat just for a minute to combine.

With a sharp serrated knife, slice the dacquoise lengthwise into thirds. Set the first layer onto a wire rack that's set over a rimmed baking sheet. Brush it with Cognac, if using. Spread over the vanilla buttercream, then press on the second layer. Again, brush it with Cognac, but this time, spread over the praline buttercream. Brush the last layer, then place it soaked-side down onto the top of the cake. Neaten the sides, filling any gaps. You want it to be as flush as possible before pouring over the ganache. Firm in the refrigerator for 15 or so minutes, just so that the chocolate clings a little easier when it goes on.

Pour the remaining ganache over the cake and slick it out with an offset palette knife so that it drips down the sides. Let it settle, then smooth. The more it's worked, the more it'll lose shine, so be decisive with your movements. Adorn with the last of the praline to patch—if you wish.

Serve the cake slightly chilled, slices cut with a warm knife. It's rich, and there will likely be leftovers. Store, loosely covered, in the refrigerator for 3 days.

the sixth sense

It's fabled that the original cake needs a day of rest before serving. I can't ever wait that long, and I won't bat a lash if you can't either. Just know that the longer it sits, the more the flavors meld and deepen, the once distinct layers becoming one.

Miso Peanut Sesame Cookies

FOR THE COOKIES

2¼ cups (280 g) all-purpose flour

1¼ teaspoons baking powder

¼ teaspoon Chinese five-spice powder

¾ cup (170 g) unsalted butter, softened at room temperature

½ cup (100 g) granulated sugar

¼ cup (55 g) light brown sugar

½ cup (130 g) smooth peanut butter

2 tablespoons white miso

1 teaspoon toasted sesame oil

FOR THE COATING

¼ cup (50 g) granulated sugar

¼ cup (35 g) unsalted raw peanuts

1 egg white, lightly whisked

I think of these and then of the traditional peanut cookies from my childhood. Part Chinese, part European, growing up was a collision of taste. The unorthodox inside took root, and only deepened with age. I find the same happens with umami.

The white miso here is sweet and creamy, with a subtle salt that settles into the crumb. The peanut butter achieves similar, and is vital for that melt-in-the-mouth feel. Use the processed stuff, not the natural kind.

/ *Makes 24 cookies* /

SIFT the flour, baking powder, and five-spice powder into a medium mixing bowl.

Next, in the bowl of a stand mixer that's fitted with the paddle attachment, or using handheld electric beaters, beat the butter and sugars on medium speed until pale and creamy, 3 to 5 minutes. Pause to scrape down the bowl, then add the peanut butter, miso, and oil. Beat until homogenous. Again, pause to scrape, then tip in the dry ingredients. Beat on low speed until a soft dough has formed. Scrape it onto a sheet of plastic wrap, then shape into a taut log that's about 1½ inches (4 cm) thick. Chill until firm enough to slice, about an hour.

Adjust racks to the top, middle, and bottom thirds of the oven, then preheat it to 350°F (180°C). Line three baking sheets with parchment paper.

For coating, pummel the sugar and peanuts together in a mortar and pestle.

Unwrap the dough onto a cutting board. With a pastry brush, wash it lightly with the egg white. Scatter over the peanut sugar, rolling and pressing it on to stick. Slice off ½ inch (1.3 cm) thick rounds with a sharp knife, then divide them among the prepared sheets, leaving a few inches of space apart for spreading.

Bake for 12 to 14 minutes, rotating halfway, until light golden. Stand for a few minutes on the sheets, then transfer off and onto a wire rack to cool further before serving. These are best eaten after cooling for a few hours, when the crumb has had time to firm and refine, but they're wonderful warm and soft too. They'll keep, stored in an airtight container, in a cool, dark place for 3 to 5 days.

Palm Sugar Tart

FOR THE CRUST

1¼ cups + 1 teaspoon (160 g) all-purpose flour

⅓ cup (40 g) confectioners' sugar

¼ cup (25 g) ground almonds

1 tablespoon Dutch processed cocoa powder

½ cup (1 stick/115 g) unsalted butter, cold and cut into ½-inch (1.3-cm) cubes

2 large egg yolks

1 large egg, lightly whisked with a pinch of salt, for the wash

FOR THE FILLING

9 large egg yolks

¼ teaspoon salt

2½ cups (600 ml) heavy cream

1 teaspoon vanilla extract

1 tablespoon rum, optional

½ cup (110 g) light brown sugar

2½ ounces (75 g) palm sugar, finely chopped

Nutmeg, finely grated, for the top

Flaky sea salt, for finishing

I spent a lot of time in Bali as a child. Introduced to the world, I remember the overwhelming sights, smells, sounds, and colors of the local market, the heart of the people who gave even when they needed to take, and clumps of dark, crystallized sugar wrapped up in tight parcels. Palm sugar was a treat then, it still is, and in my hands, it never lasts long. I use it to deepen this tart, which has a subtle umami characteristic that's as scorched in my mind as my palate.

/ *Serves 8* /

For the crust, whisk together the flour, confectioners' sugar, almonds, and cocoa powder in a large mixing bowl. Add the butter and toss to coat. Begin to rub and blend the cubes into the dry ingredients until mostly pebble-sized pieces remain. Add the yolks and stir with a wooden spoon to combine. It will seem clumpy but hold when pinched. Bring the dough together into a ball, then shape it into a disc. Cover with plastic wrap and chill for at least an hour.

Position a 10-inch (25-cm) tart tin that's 1.3 inches (3.5 cm) deep with a removable base onto a baking sheet. Unwrap the dough onto a floured work surface and lightly dust the top. With a pin, roll it into a circle that's about ⅛ inch (.3 cm) thick, or a few inches larger than the tin that you're using. Transfer and fit, then trim off the excess overhang. Freeze while the oven preheats to 350°F (180°C).

Line the crust with a sheet of parchment paper, then fill it to the brim with ceramic weights or dried beans. Bake for 20 minutes, or until dry and set. Cool slightly, then remove the weights. Coat thinly with egg wash. Return to the oven and continue to bake for another 8 to 10 minutes, until golden. Transfer to a wire rack and leave to cool. Lower the temperature to 265°F (130°C).

Next, make the filling. In a medium heatproof bowl, whisk together the yolks and salt. Pour the cream, vanilla, and rum, if using, into a large saucepan. Bring to a simmer over medium heat. Meanwhile, put the sugars into a separate saucepan. Heat over medium-high heat, shaking the pan often, until the granules have transformed into a deeply caramelized liquid. It shouldn't take longer than a few minutes—don't abandon it. Immediately add into the warmed cream. It'll sputter as it's added, so be cautious. Lower the heat and stir softly to integrate, then stream it all into the yolks, whisking until well combined.

Strain the filling through a fine-mesh sieve into the crust, slowly, as to avoid the creation of small bubbles. If they do rise to the surface, prick them.

Bake for 30 to 35 minutes, until just set but still with a slight wobble. Cool on a wire rack, then transfer to the refrigerator to chill completely. Finish the tart with nutmeg and salt before serving. This will keep, loosely covered, in the refrigerator for 2 to 3 days.

Vin Jaune Sabayon

FOR THE SABAYON

4 large egg yolks

⅓ cup (70 g) granulated sugar

Zest and juice from ½ a lemon

⅔ cup (160 ml) vin jaune

FOR THE STRAWBERRIES

1 pound (450 g) strawberries, hulled

⅓ cup (70 g) granulated sugar

A pinch of fennel pollen, optional

2 tablespoons vin jaune

Juice from ½ a lemon

1 cup (240 ml) heavy cream

Vin jaune is something of a fable. The wine, made from Savagnin, is created under stringent gaze in the Jura region. It's elusive, desirable, and obscure, made sous voile–style, where the liquid is aged under a veil of yeast to produce its oxidatively unctuous character. It lends a nutty depth to this saucy-custard-like dessert, with a striking acid line to carry the richness through. If you can't find vin jaune (again, elusive), another dry white wine will also work, but try to seek it out. The bottles are small but potent.

/ *Serves 4* /

For the sabayon, put the egg yolks, sugar, lemon zest and juice, and vin jaune into a medium heatproof bowl, then set it over a saucepan that's filled with a few inches of barely simmering water. Do not let the base of the bowl touch the water below. Heat over medium-low heat until airy and thick, whisking slowly in concentric movements to ease it along. It should take 6 to 8 minutes and hold a trail if you run your finger through it, like curd. Strain into a medium heatproof bowl through a fine-mesh sieve, then cover the surface with plastic wrap. Chill thoroughly.

Preheat the oven to 425°F (220°C). Toss together the strawberries, sugar, and fennel pollen, if using, in a medium mixing bowl, then add the vin jaune and lemon juice. Transfer into a roasting dish. Roast for 20 to 25 minutes, turning the fruit halfway through, until tender and caramelized. Remove and cool completely.

Just before you're ready to serve, in the bowl of a stand mixer that's fitted with the whisk attachment, whip the cream to supple peaks on medium speed. Remove the sabayon from the refrigerator and give it a gentle stir to awaken. Fold in the whipped cream. Spoon into your desired vessels, and then top with the strawberries. Eat cold, soon after. Leftovers will keep, covered, in the refrigerator for 2 to 3 days.

the sixth sense

Sabayon is pure voluptuousness. It transforms any fruit into an elegant dessert and can be served warm straight off the stove, or cold with cream folded through it, as I do here. I like to experiment with it, though—from the alcohol to the fruit and its herbaceous accompaniment, it exists as a foundation for the senses and should be treated as such.

Aged Parmesan Kipferl

1 cup (2 sticks/230 g) unsalted butter, softened at room temperature

½ cup + 2 tablespoons (130 g) granulated sugar

2 large egg yolks, cold

¼ teaspoon almond extract

2½ cups (315 g) all-purpose flour

1 cup + 3 tablespoons (115 g) ground almonds

⅓ cup (35 g) finely grated aged parmesan cheese

Confectioners' sugar

Kipferl refers to the curvature of these crescent cookies in Austrian. They're something my grandparents would bake for the holidays each year, and though dusted in sugar, were never too sweet. I think of them, and then of these, and home.

The parmesan delivers the taste I remember. It creates an arresting pull that's important not just for flavor, but also structure. It sharpens the sweet, crumbles the texture, and gives off a lovely golden hue. A bite will shift as time goes on, so your feelings about these cookies in one moment won't be the same in the next.

/ ***Makes 50 cookies*** /

In the bowl of a stand mixer that's fitted with the paddle attachment, or using handheld electric beaters, beat the butter and sugar together until pale and creamy. We're not looking to incorporate too much air, just enough so that the ingredients are mingled—a few minutes should do. Add the yolks, one at a time, followed by the almond extract. Pause to scrape down the bowl, then resume on low speed, beating in the flour and almonds. Beat in the parmesan cheese until evenly distributed throughout the dough. Cover with plastic wrap and chill until firm enough to handle, about an hour.

Adjust racks to the top and bottom thirds of the oven, then preheat it to 350°F (180°C). Line two baking sheets with parchment paper.

Lightly dust a work surface with flour. Portion out the dough into mounds that are about ½ ounce (15 g) in weight, or a generous teaspoon. Roll each into a smooth ball and then a log, pinching to form a horseshoe-like U shape. Flour as needed to prevent sticking. Divide between the prepared sheets, leaving a few inches of space apart for spreading.

Bake for 10 to 12 minutes, rotating halfway through, until light golden. Remove and transfer to a wire rack. Cool completely, then dust liberally with confectioners' sugar before serving. I think these are best eaten a few days after making, when tender, almost disintegrating. Seal in an airtight container and store in a cool, dark place for 3 to 5 days.

the sixth sense

Sometimes the awareness of cheese in these cookies, however slight, is a mental block to experiencing their delight in their full. I aim to please my eater, and tailor accordingly. Vanillekipferl are the traditional kind. Incorporating a whole, fleshy vanilla bean instead of the parmesan would be a sweeter substitute—or make it bitter by throwing in ⅓ cup (45 g) cocoa nibs.

Porcini Crêpe Cake

The thought of porcini in dessert might seem provocative, but the taste isn't. It's warm, rich, and grounding, the mushrooms offering an unmistakable funk that adds weight to this cake. The caliber of chocolate here makes all the difference—porcini are potent and demand an equal. To test, push a square to the roof of your mouth and let it melt. How the chocolate reveals itself will determine whether it should be used.

/ *Serves 8* /

FOR THE CRÊPES

1¾ cups + 2 teaspoons (225 g) all-purpose flour

⅔ cup (50 g) Dutch processed cocoa powder

¼ cup (50 g) granulated sugar

4 large eggs

1 tablespoon rum, optional

2½ cups (600 ml) whole milk

⅓ cup (75 g) unsalted butter, melted

FOR THE CRÈME DIPLOMATE

2¼ teaspoons (6 g) powdered gelatin

2¼ cups (540 ml) whole milk

1 teaspoon porcini powder

6 large egg yolks

½ cup (100 g) granulated sugar

¼ cup (32 g) cornstarch

¾ cup + 2 tablespoons (150 g) finely chopped dark chocolate

2 tablespoons unsalted butter

¾ cup + 2 tablespoons (210 ml) heavy cream

1 teaspoon vanilla extract

Unsalted butter, for cooking the crêpes

For the crêpes, sift the flour and cocoa powder into a large mixing bowl. Stir in the sugar. Push the ingredients aside to form a well, then add the eggs and rum, if using. Stream in the milk, whisking slowly until combined. Whisk in the butter. Pass the batter into a separate bowl through a fine-mesh sieve. Cover with plastic wrap and leave to rest overnight in the refrigerator.

Next, prepare the crème diplomate. Put 2 tablespoons cold water into a small bowl and sprinkle in the gelatin. Stir to incorporate with something small and sharp, like a toothpick, and set aside to bloom. Meanwhile, put the milk and porcini powder into a large saucepan that's set over medium heat. In a medium heatproof bowl, whisk together the yolks, sugar, and cornstarch. When the milk has come to a simmer, stream a little of it into the yolks, whisking softly to incorporate. Transfer back into the pan that's set on the stove. Continue to heat, whisking constantly, until smooth and thick. A few stray bubbles should break the surface. Remove and whisk in the gelatin, followed by the chocolate and butter. Strain into a large heatproof bowl, then cover the surface with plastic wrap. Chill in the refrigerator, also overnight.

The next morning, cook the crêpes. Remove the batter and give it a stir to awaken. Set an 8½-inch (22-cm) crêpe pan over medium heat and slick it with enough butter. Stream in a scant ⅓ cup batter, raising, tilting, and swirling the pan as you pour, so that a thin film lines the base. Cook for 2 minutes, then flip and cook on the other side for another minute or so more, until light golden. Transfer to a plate. Wipe out the pan and re-butter. Repeat with the remaining batter, stacking a sheet of parchment paper between the layers as you go. You should have about 16 crêpes in total. Cool completely.

In the bowl of a stand mixer that's fitted with the whisk attachment, whip the cream and vanilla to soft peaks on medium speed. In a separate

bowl, whip the crème diplomate until smooth. Fold in a third of the whipped cream to loosen it, followed by another third, and then the last.

To assemble, place a crêpe onto a serving plate. Spread with a few tablespoons of the filling, almost to the edges. Lay over the next crêpe, then spread again. Repeat this process until the final crêpe has been laid. Loosely cover, then refrigerate until firm, at least an hour.

When you're ready to serve, slice the cake with a sharp knife to reveal the distinct layers. It's best eaten within 2 to 3 days and should be kept, loosely covered, in the refrigerator.

Truffle Tiramisu

2 cups (480 g) mascarpone

½ cup (120 ml) heavy cream

¼ to ½ teaspoon truffle paste, to taste

Seeds scraped from 1 vanilla bean

¾ cup + 2 tablespoons (175 g) granulated sugar

5 large egg yolks

1 cup (240 ml) espresso

⅓ cup (80 ml) coffee liqueur

About 24 savoiardi biscuits or ladyfingers

Dutch processed cocoa powder, to finish

the sixth sense

If it aligns, a fine grating of truffle over the top would not go astray.

Also known as a lover's end. I return to this recipe often, and each time it gets better, deeper, stronger, and more powerful.

Truffles come with a cost, literal or implied, and the preciousness of them makes any inclusion special. Odorous as well as amorous, even a small amount can be sensed, and they should be used sparingly, with restraint. Imbued into the cream, the truffle softens the edge of this bittersweet tiramisu. For ease as well as access, I use a paste for the recipe. Look for one that's pure. A lot seem like that on the surface but aren't—containing exuberant salt, alliums, or other fungi to bolster.

/ *Serves 8 to 12* /

In the bowl of a stand mixer that's fitted with the whisk attachment, whisk the mascarpone, cream, truffle paste, vanilla seeds, and 2 tablespoons of the sugar to soft peaks on medium speed, being cautious not to overdo it, as you don't want it to be resistant when folding later on. Keep cold until needed.

Next, combine the remaining ¾ cup (150 g) sugar with ¼ cup (60 ml) water in a deep saucepan. Bring to a boil over medium heat, then raise the heat to high. Continue to cook until it reaches 250°F (120°C) on a candy thermometer. Meanwhile, start whisking the yolks in a stand mixer that's set on medium speed. As soon as the syrup is at temperature, remove from the heat and slowly pour it into the whisking yolks. Raise the speed medium-high. Continue to whisk until pale, thick, and voluminous, 4 to 6 minutes. It should flow softly back onto itself in a ribbonlike trail when the whisk is lifted. Fold in the cream mixture.

In a shallow bowl, stir together the espresso and liqueur.

Slick the base of a 4-cup (1-L) capacity dish with a layer of the cream. Swirl a savoiardi into the espresso liquid until almost drenched, then position it into the dish. Repeat, using enough biscuits to form a foundational bottom layer. Cover with half of the cream. Top with a second round of biscuits, still soaking and then nestling them into the soft beneath. Blanket with the last of the cream. Dust with cocoa to coat.

Transfer the tiramisu to the refrigerator and let it rest for at least 8 hours, but preferably overnight. It's best with time, the flavors melded, knowing each other.

Spoon and serve, generously. It will keep, loosely covered, in the refrigerator for 2 to 3 days.

Baci di Dama

FOR THE COOKIES

1 cup (140 g) hazelnuts

1¼ cups + 1 tablespoon (165 g) all-purpose flour

⅓ cup + 1 teaspoon (35 g) ground almonds

1 teaspoon porcini powder

¼ teaspoon salt

½ cup + 1 tablespoon (115 g) granulated sugar

½ cup (1 stick/115 g) unsalted butter, cold and cut into ½-inch (1.3-cm) cubes

FOR THE FILLING

½ cup (85 g) chopped gianduja or milk chocolate

Soft, tender, and disintegrating, the Rubenesque stature of baci di dama, or lady's kisses, makes them rife for play. Hazelnuts are traditional, with their warm and sweet profile that's also slightly suggestive of cocoa. The use of porcini is less common but not misplaced. The coming together of the two leaves an impression that deepens with time. These are a vision.

/ *Makes 25 cookies* /

PREHEAT the oven to 350°F (180°C).

Line a baking sheet with parchment paper and scatter the hazelnuts into an even layer over it. Roast until fragrant, 8 to 10 minutes, then remove and cool completely. Grind to a coarse meal in a food processor. Tip it into a large mixing bowl, along with the flour, almonds, porcini powder, and salt. Stir in the sugar.

Add the butter and toss to coat. With your fingertips, begin to rub and blend the cubes into the dry ingredients until the mixture resembles breadcrumbs. Knead to bring the dough together into a ball. Cover with plastic wrap and chill for at least an hour.

Adjust racks to the top, middle, and bottom thirds of the oven, then preheat it to 300°F (150°C). Line three baking sheets with parchment paper.

Remove the dough from the refrigerator. Using a generous teaspoon as a measure, portion it into little mounds that weigh about .35 ounce (10 g) each. Roll them into smooth balls with the palm of your hands and then divide among the prepared sheets, leaving a few inches of space apart for spreading.

Bake for 16 to 18 minutes, rotating halfway through, until light golden, crackled, and dry to the touch. Remove and cool completely on the sheets.

When you're ready to fill, put the gianduja or milk chocolate into a medium heatproof bowl, then set it over a saucepan filled with a few inches of barely simmering water. Do not let the base of the bowl touch the water below. Stir over medium-low heat until melted. Cool on the kitchen counter until thickened to a spreadable consistency.

Transfer the cookies onto a wire rack. Turn half of them over, flat side facing up. They're fragile, so handle with care. Working one by one, pipe or dollop the melted chocolate into the middles. Sandwich with a mate, applying pressure to spread the filling to the edges. Lay them on their sides and leave to set.

These are best eaten after a few days of rest. Store in an airtight container in a cool, dark place.

Index

Note: Page references in *italics* indicate photographs.

C

d

e

f

g

t

u

v

w

y

HarperCollins books may be purchased for educational, business, or sales promotional use. For information, please email the Special Markets Department at SPsales@harpercollins.com.

hc.com

FIRST EDITION

Designed by Tai Blanche
Photography by Thalia Ho

Library of Congress Cataloging-in-Publication Data has been applied for.

ISBN 978-0-06-341141-8

Printed in Malaysia

26 27 28 29 30 PCA 10 9 8 7 6 5 4 3 2 1